IMPOSSIBLE
COMMANDS

HOW TO OBEY GOD WHEN IT
SEEMS THAT YOU CAN'T

Impossible Commands
© Jonathan Allcock, 2019

Published by
The Good Book Company

thegoodbook.com | thegoodbook.co.uk
thegoodbook.com.au | thegoodbook.co.nz | thegoodbook.co.in

A CIP catalogue record for this book is available from the British Library.

ISBN: 9781784983338 | Printed in the UK

Design by André Parker

Contents

Introduction:
An impossible dream?

Imagine a life where obeying God was a source of deep and satisfying joy. Imagine a life where obedience was not a burden, but instead became the desire and longing of our hearts.

Does that sound like an impossible dream?

It might surprise you to know that this is the sort of life the Bible encourages us to pursue. God sets before us a life of joyful (not miserable) obedience. That's why you find people saying things like this to the Lord:

> *Your statutes are wonderful;*
> *therefore I obey them.*   *(Psalm 119 v 129)*

Obedience is driven by a joyful wonder at the goodness of God's commands. The writer of this psalm doesn't obey because he has to. He obeys because he wants to.

But I'm probably not alone in finding that my experience of obedience is not often like that.

Yes, I know that I'm supposed to obey God—but that's where it ends. It's something I'm *supposed* to do.

Like taking regular exercise, eating healthy food and going to the dentist.

I know I should do those things, but they're not high on my "things-that-bring-me-joy" list. I try to avoid them. I put them off as long as possible. And when guilt gets the better of me, I do the bare minimum required. So I find excuses, or I redefine the rules so that "healthy food" means drinking Diet Coke instead of Regular, and only eating cake on days with a "y" in their name.

Many Christians live their lives feeling they should obey God, so they try to obey God but find it impossible. That either leaves us feeling crushed and guilty or we work hard at excuses and at redefining the rules to avoid that nagging guilt.

You probably don't need me to tell you that this is a profoundly unjoyful way of life. We can quickly get ourselves into a mindset where we define ourselves as "failing" in the area of obeying God. We can be pretty pessimistic and negative about ourselves. God's commands just make us feel bad.

This book is about obedience—but not that sort of obedience.

I want to invite you to rethink why we obey and how we obey. It would be great to be asking God to move obedience from the category labelled "supposed to" and transfer it to the category labelled "want to", and from "can't" to "will".

That is what we need. Not simply a change in our behaviour but a change in our desires.

We're going to see that obedience really matters. It's no good shrugging our shoulders and using God's grace as an excuse to ignore the reality of sin. God saves us for obedience. But we have to know what sort of obedience he has saved us for.

Imagine you're working on a ship. You're slaving away in the engine room, where it's hot and the diesel fumes fill your lungs. The pounding of machinery fills your ears and drowns out every other sound. You can hardly breathe and feel yourself suffocating.

Isn't that what obedience to God can often feel like?

It doesn't have to be that way. I want to invite you to leave the engine room and head up to the deck. We need to take a deep breath and fill our lungs with the beautiful grace of God. Breathe in his love and forgiveness. Fix your gaze on Jesus, the One who died to pay for our disobedience. Feel his mercy and approval.

There is a way to obey God's commands and enjoy it. And it starts with realising that when you think those commands sound impossible, you're right—they are impossible.

1. By impossible,
I mean impossible

There are some things in life that are hard.

It would be hard to fit a camel in the back of a medium-sized family car. It would take some effort, a bit of sweat and a whole lot of determination. But I reckon it could be done. I confess I've never tried, but it's not out of the question.

That's not what this book is about. We're not talking about something that is hard.

A camel through the eye of a needle? That's a whole different ball game. It's well beyond the reach not just of reality but also the wildest stretch of human imagination. Even the most optimistic and enthusiastic camel contortionist is not going to attempt that one.

That is what this book is about. We're talking about something that is absolutely and utterly impossible. Completely beyond the reach of human ability. I know it sounds strange, but if we're ever going to find joy in our obedience, it really does start here. Obedience to God's commands is impossible for us.

In Mark chapter 10, Jesus used this dramatic image to help his disciples understand what it meant to follow him. He said:

> *It is easier for a camel to go through the eye of a needle than for someone who is rich to enter the kingdom of God.* (Mark 10 v 25)

Jesus wasn't just saying it's hard: he was saying it's impossible. Until we face up to this impossibility, we will be stuck in an endless cycle of effort, sweat, determination and disappointment.

Yes, we can
There is something in us that doesn't like to be told that things are impossible. We live in a "can-do" culture with a whole generation that have grown up being told they can do whatever they want.

Numerous voices tell us constantly that there is no such thing as "impossible". You can do whatever you want to do, and you can be whatever you want to be. I went to a primary-school assembly a few years ago to watch one of my children sing. The whole class sang beautifully, with beaming faces.

With eager hearts they told us that they could do anything—absolutely anything—just so long as they believed in themselves.

This is the culture we're living in. On the surface it seems positive and lovely, but in reality it's devastating. It simply is not true. When we fail, it is our fault. After all, we had the power—we just should have believed more.

We have all heard the Olympic athlete who has just won gold saying something like, "This proves that anyone can do anything if they just believe".

But, of course, it doesn't prove that. For the one winner, there are hundreds who have failed. Hundreds who have dedicated their lives to pursuing the Olympic dream and have fallen short.

And many of us approach the Christian life with exactly this mindset. We think that we should be able to obey God's commands if we just try hard enough.

So we spend our lives trying to shove the metaphorical camel in the back of the metaphorical car—and feeling euphoric when we make some progress and worthless when the hump is still sticking out the window.

We think we can do it. We're told we can do it. We know we're supposed to be able to do it. If we aren't able to do it, there is something wrong with us. So we all pretend we are doing it when deep down we know we aren't.

That is the madness of our lives. It is the slavery of the impossible.

No, we can't

Only Jesus can break this endless cycle. He is far more blunt with us. When it comes to God and his kingdom, we can't "do it". We just can't. No matter how much we try and how hard we push, the camel won't go through the eye of that needle. We convince ourselves it must be possible; we think that perhaps we are the exception. We aren't.

We imagine that if we just try a bit harder, we can obey God, please God and enter his kingdom.

But we can't.

"Impossible" is a word that must be part of our Christian vocabulary. I'm not talking about a defeatist, small-minded negativity. I'm talking about a realistic and resolute honesty. And here is why this matters so much: *it's only when you embrace the impossibility that you are standing right on the very edge of true freedom.*

After Jesus has explained that it is impossible for us, do you know what he says next? Jesus does not say that it is impossible—and therefore you might as well give up trying. He does not say that impossibility leads to defeat. Instead, he utters these deeply profound and magnificent words:

> *With man this is impossible, but not with God; all things are possible with God.* (Mark 10 v 27)

"Honestly facing up to the impossibility of my own obedience leads me not to despair but to the God who is able to do all things."

———————

IMPOSSIBLE
COMMANDS

There it is: there is the true freedom of what it means to be a Christian. Honestly facing up to the impossibility of my own obedience leads me not to despair but to the God who is able to do all things.

That is true for getting started on the Christian life, and it is true for every act of obedience we take in following Jesus. Many of our problems in living for Jesus stem from the root problem that we think we can do it. We think that we have the power within us. We set about trying to push the camel. In this book we're going to see that understanding the impossibility is the first step to obedience.

A man who thinks he can
Let's back up a bit and see what has led up to Jesus using such a striking image.

It starts with a man. Mark doesn't tell us any more than that at the start of the story. In verse 17 he simply introduces us to "a man".

> As Jesus started on his way, a man ran up to him and fell on his knees before him. "Good teacher," he asked, "what must I do to inherit eternal life?"
>
> *(Mark 10 v 17)*

The man gets a couple of things very right.

He wants to know what he needs to do to be part of God's great kingdom. It's good that he's bothered about God's kingdom—he can see that it really matters. God is bringing all things in this world together under his appointed King, Jesus. That is God's plan for the world, and this anonymous man wants to know how to get in on it.

And it is good that he comes to Jesus. Clearly he has understood that there is something about Jesus that is significant.

The man cares about the right thing. He comes to the right place.

But this man has got one thing very wrong. He wants to know what he has to do. He has a high view of his own ability. He has a lot of confidence in his power to obey.

So that is where Jesus starts.

> *"Why do you call me good?" Jesus answered. "No one is*
> *good—except God alone. You know the commandments:*
> *'You shall not murder, you shall not commit adultery,*
> *you shall not steal, you shall not give false testimony,*
> *you shall not defraud, honour your father and mother.'"*
> *(Mark 10 v 18-19)*

Jesus points the man to God as the ultimate standard of good and begins to list the commandments. The man is completely unperturbed by all this.

> *Teacher ... all these I have kept since I was a boy.*
> *(Mark 10 v 20)*

He is oozing self-righteousness. What a staggering claim to make. He has worked hard; he has kept the rules; he has tried his best. It all looks good.

But Jesus sees things differently.

Love

The next sentence is key. Here it is: *Jesus looked at him and loved him.*

This is the only man in the whole of Mark's Gospel that we are explicitly told that Jesus loved. That's striking because of what the love of Jesus looks like in this story.

Jesus loves this man too much to allow him to continue in his self-deluded little world of sweat, hard work and determination. He is not willing to stroke the man's ego and tell him how wonderful he is. Instead, Jesus issues a command.

It isn't hard to understand what Jesus is saying. He isn't being vague and unspecific. But this one command undermines the whole foundation that the man has built his life on. Here's the command:

> *"One thing you lack," [Jesus] said. "Go, sell everything you have and give to the poor, and you will have treasure in heaven. Then come, follow me."* (v 21)

There is no room for negotiation or confusion. Here is what Jesus requires of this man. He must sell everything.

> *At this the man's face fell. He went away sad, because*
> *he had great wealth.* (v 22)

The man slowly turns around and starts to walk away. Only at this point in the story does Mark tell us the critical piece of information about this man—he had great wealth.

It's a very poignant moment. Jesus loves the man— and he lets him walk away. Does that surprise you? Jesus doesn't chase after the man and lower the bar. He doesn't negotiate and settle on a figure that the man will be willing to give.

Jesus demands it all. That is the command, and there is no budging.

It is an impossible command. It's not just hard. We're not in the realm of squeezing camels into cars. No, it was impossible. And it was supposed to be.

The bar is too high

Why would Jesus set the bar so impossibly high? Why would Jesus demand something that cannot be done? Not because he is cruel and harsh, but precisely because he loves this man.

The man had reduced God's commands to something he could achieve. He had a view of God's word that meant its commands were within his power. *Yes, I can do that.*

But now he was confronted with something absolutely beyond him. The command Jesus issued was not supposed to make the man say, "Yes that's fine. I can do that. I will go and give everything away."

Instead, the command Jesus issued that day was designed to expose the truth that the man could not do what he thought he could do. His heart was absolutely captivated by money. His money was his god. He was held powerfully in its grip. Jesus knew that and, because he loved this man, he wanted the man to know it too. It would be such a mistake to think that Jesus was expecting this man to go and do what he said. That was not the intention of the command.

The right response to the command would be to fall on his knees and, with a quivering voice, speak the words, "I can't do it". Only then, with his self-confidence in tatters and his heart exposed, would he be ready to receive the kingdom of God like a little child (Mark 10 v 15).

I can't do it

They are such hard words for us to say. But they are essential words for the Christian to learn. Our natural inclination to say, "I can" needs to be exposed. Our self-confident hearts need to be challenged. Not because Jesus is harsh and unkind—he is never that—but precisely because he looks at us and loves us.

Jesus loves us far too much to stroke our egos and tell us how fabulous we are. Instead, he issues commands that are far beyond our ability to obey *in order to drive us to him.*

The first step in learning to obey God is to understand with absolute crystal clarity that I CAN'T do it. I can't obey God. (By the way, before you close this book and give up, this is not the only step. We're going to see that we can begin to obey God. There are more steps to come, but it starts here.)

We aren't supposed to take the commands of God and work out a strategy for how we can make them doable. If we try that, we will inevitably shrink his commands, and, rather than obeying him, we will obey our reworking of his commands so that we can pat ourselves on the back and feel good about our obedience. That is classic man-made religion, and it is deeply offensive to God.

The commands of God are not to be approached with a self confident "can-do" attitude. When we come across God's commands, we will find they are always far beyond our natural ability to obey.

Rather than freak out, or try and find a loophole, or re-interpret the command in a more "realistic" way, we need to let Jesus confront us with the sheer impossibility.

Think back to what Jesus said to that rich young man.

When he says, "Go, sell everything you have and give to the poor," we can very quickly find our reaction becoming, *Of course he doesn't mean I should do that. That would be ridiculous and impractical. He was just talking to that man. He just means I should be more generous. Yes, I think I can manage to be a bit more generous. I will try and give a bit more money this week. Great—well done me.*

No, that is precisely the problem. We think we can do it. We find a solution to the problem of obeying the commands—but we aren't obeying him at all.

Instead, stop and feel the weight of the commands Jesus gives. Feel the way money holds a power over your heart. Let the very commands of Jesus expose you. Every command found in the pages of the Bible will have that effect on us if we stop and listen. Don't run from that. It doesn't feel comfortable; it doesn't give us a warm, fuzzy feeling about how great we are—but it is there, in that place of weakness, that we will truly learn to whisper these two words: *I can't.*

And that honours God more than you will ever know. It is the first step on the road to joyful, deep and satisfying obedience.

Only the first step...

2. Lazarus,
come out

On the London Underground train network there are three rails that the trains run along. Two of them are for the wheels of the train—this is pretty standard train-track procedure. But then there is the third rail. This is the rail that carries the power to make the train move. Without the third rail the train isn't going anywhere. It will simply sit in the station. The track stretches out into the distance offering a world of opportunity, but without any power the train simply cannot realise its potential.

What is the third rail in the life of the Christian? When we decide to trust and follow Jesus, we discover that he sets out before us a whole new life to be lived. A new direction, new priorities, new commands to obey, new tracks for our lives to run along.

But where does the power come from to obey God's commands and live this new life? That's what we're exploring in this chapter. It is crucial to our view of obedience.

Mind the gap

We sometimes drive a wedge between the gospel and obedience. We see over and over again in the pages of the Bible that Jesus saves us (which he does), not because we obey God's rules (which we can't) but because of his grace (which is awesome). For example, it's crystal clear in Titus 3:

> *He [God] saved us, not because of righteous things we had done, but because of his mercy.*
>
> *(Titus 3 v 5)*

But all of this means that we can get very confused about what obedience is and why it matters. Do I need to obey God's commands or not?

Where does obedience fit in? The danger is that we assume that obedience is our part of the bargain. God saves us, and then, to show him how thankful we are, we try really hard to keep his commands. We have this sense that we really ought to obey him after all he has done for us.

But when we try to obey, we find we can't, and so we can end up feeling desperately guilty.

The commands of God feel as if they're against us. They are words that sit there on a page condemning us and pointing out our failure. We feel useless as we read them only to find ourselves back in the relentless cycle of trying desperately to find some way to obey. It's hard to get excited about obedience.

It can seem as if God's commands are the two rails that show me how I'm supposed to live, but I'm utterly lacking in power to get the train moving. We can quickly become resentful of God's commands.

Does that sound familiar?

The third rail

But what if the commands of God are more than that? What if the commands of God are not just rules but actually *part* of the good life God has for us? What if these words are not just dead letters on a page but are living and powerful to bring about real change? What if the power to obey is found within the commands themselves?

That would be a game-changer. That would lead to a completely different view of God's word. Perhaps we might even begin to discover the reality of a joyful obedience.

It would begin to make sense of why the writer of Psalm 119 can say:

> *Oh, how I love your law!*   (Psalm 119 v 97)

This is going to require us to think hard about the nature of God and his words. Here is the big idea we're going to try to get our heads around:

For a follower of Jesus, the commands of God come accompanied with the power to bring about the obedience they command.

I realise that might sound like an odd way to phrase it, but don't let that put you off. In reality, I'm not saying anything very strange at all. It's the same as saying that God gives us the power to obey his commands. Or that the Holy Spirit is the one who empowers our obedience. The third rail is not to be found in ourselves but in *God*.

But I do want to press home that there is something about the very commands themselves that should give us great hope. This matters because I think we often feel as if God's words are against us. They condemn us. They are opposed to us.

Rules

After all, that's our normal experience of rules. Speed limits on the roads, rules in sport, and the complex tax laws we have to obey—all of them are sitting there waiting for us to step out of line so they can condemn us. So it is very natural to see God's commands in precisely the same way.

And let's be clear—*before we come to Jesus,* God's commands really do work like that.

God's law does show up our sin. It does reveal how often we fail. It does highlight how much we deserve punishment, and how much we need Jesus.

When people refuse to obey God's word, that doesn't mean it is powerless and failing. It is doing what God intended and exposing the problem in our heart. It stands against us.

God's law makes it very obvious that we cannot save ourselves—no matter how hard we try.

Only Jesus has lived the life of perfect obedience, and so only Jesus can save us. He willingly walked to the cross, where he died for our failure. He took the punishment for our disobedience. Our hope rests not in *our* obedience but in *his*. We are saved not as we obey the rules but as we trust in him. He obeyed all of God's law *for* us and his perfect record of obedience is counted by God as ours. Not only does he forgive all our sin, but he gives us his perfect righteousness. Our obedience adds nothing. It never could and it doesn't need to.

But when we are saved by God, a remarkable change in the function of God's law occurs. Here is the critical thing for our obedience: when we become God's children by faith, the commands of God take on a whole new nature. Rather than being a constant reminder of our abject failure and standing against us, they become the loving words of the Father who is *for* us.

Now God's commands are accompanied by God's power to enable our obedience.

We need to think that over a bit more carefully to see what is going on.

Words of power
God's words are not like my words. My words have very limited power.

When I give a command, it expresses my desire. But often my command is absolutely powerless to bring about what I commanded.

This is extremely clear to me in my role as a father. When my children were small, I would issue a command. "Please put your shoes on." The command expressed a very real (and increasingly urgent, even verging on desperate) desire. I really wanted my children to put their shoes on. But my words had no power to bring about the shoe-putting-on event. There is an inherent weakness built into my human words.

God's words are just not like that. God's words come with power. God does not simply express a desire that requires an external power to bring that event into being. The very command itself is the power of God to bring change.

To put it another way, God is not a frustrated parent sitting in heaven telling his children to put their shoes on and desperately hoping they might find a way to obey him. That is not the God of the Bible. Yes, it's true that we do act like naughty children, refusing to listen to God— but it would be a huge mistake to therefore figure that God's words are as powerless as mine. There is something much bigger going on. The problem is certainly not a lack of power in God's command.

Think about the very start of the Bible. Creation starts with a command: "Let there be light". When God issued that command, he was not expressing a general desire that

"Every command you read in the Bible should cause hope to rise within you as you call out to your Father for the power to obey."

IMPOSSIBLE
COMMANDS

someone somewhere out there would turn some lights on. He was not laying down two rails hoping that the power to make things happen would appear from somewhere.

His command was accompanied by his power to bring about light. This is majestic. As God commanded, so it came to be.

> *And God said, "Let there be light," and there was light.*
> *(Genesis 1 v 3)*

There was no external power required—the word of God did it all. Light did not have to get its own shoes on. The command of God was enough to get the work done.

This is what God's commands are like. They really do have power to get things done.

Unlimited power

Why do God's words have that quality? At the risk of stating the obvious, it's because they are the words of God.

My words are *my* words and therefore have limited power. They can do some things, but often they fail because I do not have the power.

God's words are *God's* words and therefore are unlimited in their power. You cannot separate words from the person speaking them. Words are an extension of who we are, and so it is with God.

If God's word ever failed, it would mean that God had failed. He would no longer be God.

This is a very big deal.

Psalm 33 puts it this way:

> *By the word of the LORD the heavens were made,*
> *their starry host by the breath of his mouth.*
>
> *(Psalm 33 v 6)*

Notice that the power to make the heavens is attributed to the word of God. There is power in the command of the King. But that isn't all. In the second half of the verse, the creative power is also associated with the breath of his mouth. The word for breath in Hebrew is the same word as Spirit. So the Spirit of God, who was "hovering over the waters" in Genesis 1 v 2, is the powerful Spirit who creates this world.

When you put all this together, you discover that God's word has power precisely because the Spirit of God is at work through that breathed-out word. God's Spirit is the power that accompanies God's word and achieves the purposes of God.

That is what's happening in all of God's commands. Here is the third rail that makes obedience possible: God's power, accompanying his word, by the power of the Holy Spirit.

You see exactly the same thing happening in the life of Jesus...

He is dead

One day, Jesus went to the tomb of his close friend Lazarus. The man had been dead for four days. Jesus knew it. The sisters knew it. The crowds knew it.

But Jesus is about to show them something they desperately need to know. He approaches the entrance of the tomb. He tells them to remove the stone, but people are unsure. There is no life in there; there is only darkness and death. That's much better left covered. But Jesus insists, and the stone is removed.

Then Jesus issues the command:

Lazarus, come out!   (John 11 v 43)

That is an impossible command. There is no way that Lazarus can obey that command. He is dead. In one sense you could say that the command is against Lazarus. It exposes him as utterly powerless. It lays out the rails, but seems futile.

And yet Jesus issues the command. It's a powerful moment.

You can imagine the stunned silence—a few nervous coughs, shaking heads at the ridiculous words that Jesus has spoken. Lazarus can't come out—he is dead. This is awkward.

But then they hear it: they can hear that something is happening in the darkness of the tomb. Something is moving in there. At first, perhaps, they think they are imagining it—but soon it becomes undeniable as "the dead man came out" (v 44).

Wow. The command was not against Lazarus at all. It was *for* him.

All Jesus does is speak. All he does is issue a command. It is that command that has the very power to bring about that which has been commanded. The power is in the word, in the command from the lips of Jesus.

It is the same word that commanded light into existence in the beginning. It is the same word that defeated armies and split waters—the same word that raised up kings and brought down rulers.

All the power of God was concentrated into that command.

Where is the power?

Of course, you could say that the power to raise Lazarus is located in Jesus. That would absolutely be true. You could also say that the power to raise Lazarus is from the Holy Spirit. It is a repeated theme in John's Gospel (for example, John 6 v 63) that the Spirit of God gives life. But it would also be true to say that the *command* of Jesus gave life to Lazarus. The power was in his words. Jesus has the words of eternal life (John 6 v 68).

Think about how that affects our understanding of obedience. Did Lazarus obey the command? Yes. He came out. But only a fool would congratulate Lazarus for his outstanding obedience. He did obey, but the power for obedience was all located in the words that Jesus spoke.

Lazarus did not need to look within himself—which admittedly would have been tough for him to do. The word of Jesus did all the work and empowered the obedience of Lazarus. There is the third rail.

It could be you

The story of Lazarus is dramatic, but it is also the story of every single Christian. By nature we were dead in our sin, we were far away from God, we were in the darkness of death, and we could not save ourselves. At that time, God's word was not for us but stood against us. It exposed our desperate situation.

But then it all changed. The powerful command of Jesus pierced through the darkness. As we heard the word of God, we were given power to do something we could not do on our own. The Holy Spirit worked in our hearts and enabled us to obey the command:

Repent and believe the good news!   *(Mark 1 v 15)*

You can't do that. And yet, if you're a Christian today, you did. That is the miracle of becoming a Christian. It is utterly extraordinary.

As with Lazarus, it starts with an impossible command that we are empowered to obey. We don't get the credit for that. How could we? All the power was in the command of Jesus that gave us life.

And so it goes on...

We might be clear on the fact that we need a miracle to obey that first command of Jesus. But do you realise it takes a miracle every time you obey? Jesus doesn't give us new life and then hand responsibility over to us for a lifetime of trying to obey. He doesn't hand us the rule book and tell us to have a go.

No. Obedience to God's commands is still impossible in our own power. If we try to live the Christian life that way, then God's commands will remain dead rules on a page that hang over us and make us feel guilty. We can so easily disconnect the gospel from obedience. We have a go at obeying, but we make so little progress. We feel guilty. We feel as if we're letting God down. We're crushed by a continual stream of *should's* that mount up and weigh us down.

> *You should pray more.*
> *You should give more.*
> *You should tell more people about Jesus.*
> *You should...*

Added to that are the *shouldn't's* that feel just as heavy.

> *You shouldn't feel like that.*
> *You shouldn't want that.*
> *You shouldn't behave like that.*

That is not what Jesus saved us for. He absolutely did save us for obedience—but not that sort of obedience.

It is so much better than that.

Jesus has given me new life, and so the commands that once condemned me now come with the full force of God's power to enable my obedience.

The power to obey is to be found within the commands God has given. His word has power.

Or, to put that another way, the power to obey comes from God's Holy Spirit, who takes the word of God and enables me to obey.

Hope will rise

So, every command we read should cause hope to rise within us as we call out to our Father for the power to obey. That sentence was important. It is the heart of what this book is about.

Every command you read in the Bible should cause hope to rise within you as you call out to your Father for the power to obey.

Now the Christian life takes on a whole new shape. Obedience is not now a burden that I must fulfil but is an opportunity to experience God's power to enable me to do the impossible. It is not a standard that is way beyond my reach but a description of what God is doing in me by his power.

The commands of God come with a promise and power embedded within them, which means we can obey. The word of God is the third rail that enables our obedience. That power comes as the Holy Spirit accompanies the word of God and brings life. Because of this, obedience can actually become our delight.

We will still fail. We fail every time we try to obey in our own strength. We fail every time we get proud and self-reliant. We fail every time we begin to think that the commands of God are nasty and mean. We will fail when God's word is not a delight to us.

But for every time we fail there is forgiveness. The Lord Jesus had to die because we cannot fully obey. We hear his precious voice. We return to him on our knees and ask him for the power to go again.

That's a prayer he loves to answer.

3. Ride the waves

Surfing is a bit of a mystery to me. I've spent many hours trying but would hesitate to claim that I'm a surfer. I know what it feels like when you see the perfect wave coming: the sense of sheer exhilaration as you launch yourself forward and the power of the wave picks you up and carries you along. That is the dream. It has happened once or twice in my life.

But more often than not my experience is like this: I see the wave coming, I launch myself forward, I paddle as hard as I can, I get ready to leap to my feet—and the wave sweeps past me, mocking me for my sheer incompetence.

It's astonishing to me that an activity that makes some people look so effortless and cool makes me look utterly awkward and desperate. It doesn't take long for my surfing enthusiasm to become despair.

Obedience can feel like that.

Every now and again, I experience an obedience wave. I hear a talk or read something, and I feel inspired and determined to obey. I see the wave coming. I can see it's good, and so I paddle with all my might. I really try. I'm full of hope that things are going to change, and I'm ready to leap to my feet. *Yes, Lord, I will do whatever you say.* But then the wave seems to sweep by, and I'm back where I started—and nothing has changed at all.

It doesn't take long for me to become cynical and give up. Others seem to make it look easy, and yet I feel like a complete mess. I settle back down into my life with little hope that anything is seriously going to change—until I see another wave coming, my hope rises, and the cycle starts again. I don't think I'm alone in this.

God has something better planned
If you're a frustrated surfer, you will either try harder... or give up. If you're a frustrated obeyer, you will either try harder... or give up.

Some of us will approach obedience with a resolve and self-determination that we can do this. We paddle as hard as we can. We make the effort. The problem is that our arms soon get tired, our resolve runs out, and the wave sweeps by. We keep trying... and paddling... but it feels like hard work. We take pride in how hard we paddle. We cover up our failures because we like to be known for our godliness, and we have a reputation to maintain. We think of obedience as a duty.

Can you relate to this? I know I can. If so, then please hear this: *God has something so much better planned for you.* Hard work might help you to make progress on a surfboard, but hard work alone will not help you with obedience.

On the other hand, some of us approach obedience with a defeatist attitude that has abandoned any hope of seriously obeying God's commands. When we've tried and failed, we decide that there's no hope and that we're never going to change. God's commands make us feel guilty, and we know we should be trying harder. But what's the point? We watch the waves come and go, and make no attempt at all to catch them. We are in a state of "bobbing". Talks come, books go; we bob up, we bob down—and it makes very little difference. I've lost count of the number of times I've sat and prayed at the end of a church service and felt so determined to obey. But the wave seems to pass me by.

If that's you, then please hear this: *God has something so much better planned for you.*

There really is a better way.

Four steps to joy

Here are four steps that can begin to move us in the direction of joyful obedience. Please keep remembering that joy is the goal here: not simply obedience, but *joyful obedience.*

The danger of setting this out as four steps is that we might begin to think this is a technique that we can master. I so easily slip into that trap. But I'm not suggesting that obedience is a simple process of following steps.

Learning to joyfully obey God's commands is all about a relationship with the God who made us: the One who loves us—the God who enables our obedience in order that we might become the people he has created us to be.

Obedience is about our relationship with God—but these steps help us to see what that might involve and help us break down what obedience will look like in day-to-day life.

The four steps are these:

- I CAN'T (honesty about our own powerlessness)

- I'M SORRY (sorrow about our stubborn refusal)

- PLEASE HELP (hopeful calling on our heavenly Father)

- LET'S GO (getting up and starting to obey)

Here they are in a bit more detail:

Step One: I can't (honesty)
We have to start here. This was chapter 1 (page 11). This is where we are honest about ourselves and about our inability to keep God's commands. It's not easy

to be honest, but it is essential. It honours God to acknowledge our weakness. It's not enough to have an abstract and general sense of our own weakness—rather, we should be honest about the specific commands and our powerlessness to obey them. It's helpful to articulate that clearly before God.

Often the problem is that we don't even really want to obey God. We don't want to live his way. We don't love him or delight in him. Rather than just pushing on in our own willpower, it's right to speak honestly before God about where our heart is at.

We might think that the next step is to seek God's power—but something else needs to happen first. I imaginatively call it Step Two.

Step Two: I'm sorry (confession)
The fact that we *can't* obey God does not mean we're therefore not to blame.

There used to be a TV show in the UK called *Can't Cook, Won't Cook*. Two contestants came on and were given ingredients with which to make a meal. One of them lacked the *ability* to cook, and the other lacked the *willingness*. They wore hats so you knew which was which. On one side of the kitchen was "Can't Cook", and on the other, "Won't Cook".

It was classic daytime TV with a very little budget and a similar level of content.

But those two statements are interesting when it comes to obedience. Can't obey or won't obey? Which is true of us?

We've already seen that we are firmly in the "Can't Obey" camp. That's Step One.

But it would be a big mistake to therefore assume we're not to blame. We all know how the logic goes: *If I can't obey God, then how can he hold me responsible? That's not fair!*

But the Bible sees it very differently. Our inability to obey God is absolutely tied to our *refusal* to obey God. It's not simply that we can't obey God; we won't obey him either. We wear both hats—"Can't Obey" and "Won't Obey".

We are powerless victims and also defiant rebels. We need to understand both in order to make progress in obedience. This is our double identity.

The last resort

I find it hard to admit that I'm wrong. I would far rather hide my mistakes, or excuse my errors, or blame someone else (as Adam and Eve were both so quick to do, Genesis 3 v 12-13). That's a much easier way to go.

I don't think my parents taught me the great art of blame-avoidance, but I still picked it up pretty quickly. I had to. I needed it time after time. When I threw a ball and smashed the precious family heirloom, what was I supposed to do? I briefly considered admitting what I'd done and saying sorry, but instinctively I knew that hiding the evidence was a far safer course of action. I collected the pieces and buried them in a drawer. I didn't get away with it.

Have you ever stopped to think why we find it so hard to say sorry? We have no problem spotting the failings in others—that much is simple. So why do we find it so hard to see them in ourselves?

I think it's because we are absolutely committed to walking the road of self-justification. I need to prove that I am worthwhile. I need to demonstrate that my life counts. My value as a human being is tied to my performance. This is why failure is so devastating to us—it threatens our basic identity and status as a human being. Whenever we feel threatened, our natural instinct is then to protect ourselves.

This is why hiding, excusing and blaming come naturally to us. They are ways of preventing our identity from being damaged. The Bible talks about it as being "wise in our own eyes" (Proverbs 3 v 5-7; Isaiah 5 v 21). We hide from God and decide for ourselves what is right. We persuade ourselves that we're ok and that our failures aren't really our fault. We instinctively look for ways to justify ourselves and excuse our sin.

It's like a man trying to paint a straight line on a sports field. He looks down at what he is doing, and his eyes tell him that the line looks good. He flatters himself about his ability to paint lines. His work looks good in his own eyes. But someone who has their head up and is looking at the whole picture can see clearly that he has wandered all over the place.

We need a more honest assessment of ourselves.

We need to be careful, because the solution is not to start thinking we are useless. Some of us have all sorts of very negative thoughts about ourselves, but that's not the same as admitting that we're sinners. Low self-esteem is not the same as acknowledging our guilt before God. We're not supposed to be driven to self-pity, or self-loathing, or miserable introspection. That would still be living on the road of self-justification, where it is all about me and my performance.

Proverbs gives us a much better way.

> *Do not be wise in your own eyes;*
> *fear the LORD and shun evil.*   *(Proverbs 3 v 7)*

We need to learn to "fear God"—to turn our eyes away from ourselves and to lift them to God. When I see God clearly, then I can see myself clearly. When I see his beauty and perfection, I will see how far I have fallen. When I lift my head, like the man trying to paint a straight line, I can see the crookedness of my life. It leaves me nowhere to hide, and I am forced to admit the truth.

But here is the strange paradox of obedience: if we never admit we're wrong, we will never experience the joy of obedience.

"You don't need to try and win God's approval. If you're trusting in Christ, you already have it. You don't need to earn a place in his kingdom—it is already yours. Your obedience is not your side of the bargain—God has done it all."

IMPOSSIBLE
COMMANDS

The inseparable link between confession and joy
We need to learn to say (and really mean) the simple words, "I'm sorry". We need to lose the excuses. Our joy depends on it.

If we don't, our obedience will become another weapon in our great pursuit of self-justification. We will use our obedience to cover our failures. We will use our performance to avoid the guilt that we feel.

Genuine, joyful gospel-shaped obedience is only possible when you have stopped trying to justify yourself and pretend you're something that you aren't.

Confession will liberate you and set you free from the road of self-justification. You can be absolutely honest with God, not just about your past failure but about your present weakness to obey.

The Bible puts it this way:

> *If we confess our sins, he is faithful and just and will forgive us our sins and purify us from all unrighteousness.*   *(1 John 1 v 9)*

A can of worms
If you ever open a can of worms, can I give you some advice? Before you open it, make sure there's someone able to deal with the worms. Otherwise, it would be much better to keep the lid tightly shut and the worms firmly hidden.

It's the same with sin. Before you get honest and confess your sin, you need to make sure there is someone who is able to deal with what comes out. Otherwise, it would make more sense to just keep the lid on, keep smiling, keep making excuses—keep pretending that everything is ok.

This is the great news about confession. As we give up on self-justification and face up to our serious failure, as we lift our eyes to God and see the reality of our own hearts, we do not need to fear.

Sin is desperately serious, and we are undoubtedly guilty. But there is One who stands ready to forgive. There is One who will deal with our sin. There is One who stands ready to justify us.

On the cross, Jesus Christ died for all our sin. Jesus died because we won't obey God. He died because of our stubborn refusal. The punishment we deserve fell on him. When we confess our sins, they are taken far away. Here is the heart of the gospel; here is the source of all true obedience. It all starts and flows from here.

That is why the second step in gospel obedience (yes, we're still on Step Two!) is to say "I'm sorry". I'm sorry that I don't want to obey you. I'm sorry that I can't obey you. I'm sorry that sin is so attractive to me. I'm sorry that you are not the overwhelming desire of my heart. I'm sorry that I find your commands a burden. You are good, everything you say is good, your commands are good, and yet my heart can't see it. There is a serious and devastating problem in my heart. I'm sorry.

Forgiven

*If we confess our sins, he is faithful and just and
will forgive us our sins and purify us from all
unrighteousness.*   *(1 John 1 v 9)*

If you have confessed your sin, then you are forgiven.
You are justified before God. You do not have to justify
yourself. Your worth and value do not flow out of your
obedience but out of what Jesus Christ has done for you.
This is why we no longer have to flatter ourselves and
pretend everything is ok. Jesus loved you when you were
at your worst. He is able to deal with your failure.

You probably know this, but do you practise it? Is
confession a daily reality—an almost instinctive
response? If not, don't skip over this bit just because you
already know 1 John 1 v 9. Pause a moment, and drink
this in deeply.

Obedience comes from this place. You don't need to
try and win God's approval. If you're trusting in Christ,
you already have it. You don't need to earn a place in
his kingdom—it is already yours. Your obedience is
not your side of the bargain—God has done it all. You
are not paying him back, or showing your thanks. His
forgiveness is a free gift of grace. There is nothing to pay.

Instead, for those forgiven by Jesus and set free from a
road of self-justification, obedience becomes our joy and
privilege. Which brings us nicely to Step Three.

Step Three: Please help

Have a look at how Jesus described the religious leaders of his day. This is how their version of obedience worked:

> *Jesus replied, "And you experts in the law, woe to you, because you load people down with burdens they can hardly carry, and you yourselves will not lift one finger to help them."* (Luke 11 v 46)

That's what human religion feels like. There are a bunch of commands which are like heavy burdens loaded up on people's shoulders. The teachers keep making their demands, but there's not even a finger's worth of help. Obedience in that situation can only ever feel like a crushing weight that will never be lifted. We must not think that God operates that way.

This is not how obedience works for the children of God. He loves you, he gave his Son to die for you, he has forgiven all your sin. You are now his precious child. God is not simply ready to lift his finger to help you—he has promised to pour out all his power on his children when they ask. Jesus puts this so beautifully:

> *Which of you fathers, if your son asks for a fish, will give him a snake instead? Or if he asks for an egg, will give him a scorpion? If you then, though you are evil, know how to give good gifts to your children, how much more will your Father in heaven give the Holy Spirit to those who ask him!"* (Luke 11 v 11-13)

Do you realise that God is on your side? He is ready and willing to give you all the resources you require to obey his commands.

As God gives his commands, he also promises to give his Spirit to all who ask. The word of God is accompanied by the power of God to enable our obedience.

All we have to do is ask. God loves to give His Holy Spirit to his children. He really is not asking us to struggle on our own.

"I can't. I'm sorry. Please help."

But all of that leads on to Step Four.

Step Four: Let's go
There is work to be done, there is effort to be exerted, there is sweat that needs to flow. The Christian life is not a serene, effortless existence. It is a fight, a marathon, a struggle.

There are people to be loved, there is sin to be killed, there are prayers to be prayed, there is work to be done. Depending on God's power does not make us lazy. It must not make us careless. Rather, it makes us defiant in our obedience.

I remember teaching my children to play cricket. When they were very small and were not even strong enough to hold the bat on their own, what did I do? I didn't shout at them and tell them to try harder. Neither did I tell them not to bother and just to sit and watch. I stood behind them and put my hands over theirs. I told them to swing as hard as they could. As the ball was bowled, we moved together and hit the ball high into the sky. As their little face broke into a huge smile, I said, "Look how far you hit it!" Do you think our heavenly Father is any less ready to help his children?

He stands behind you and says, *Fight as hard as you can.* Then he swings his mighty arm and, together, we smack sin far into the distance.

You will often fail. You will fail to fight. You will fail to trust your Father. But sometimes you will swing and win. There is a confidence, even a defiance, in this sort of obedience. Sin will not rule over you. Sin will not ultimately defeat you.

As you work, God works. As you fight, he fights. As you win, he wins. Here is gospel-driven, joyful obedience.

The first three steps come first

So, yes, obedience is frustrating. The wave sweeps by, and nothing changes. But could that be because we are approaching Step Four of obedience without Steps One to Three?

I've never had a surfing lesson. I don't want to waste my time with that. As far as I can see, surf-school students spend most of the time lying on the beach practising the technique and learning the basics. I don't need that. I want to be in among the waves. I really should be able to manage this. So I keep paddling and splashing and failing.

Perhaps the reason the waves keep passing me by is that I want to shortcut the basics and just get on with it.

We're all like that sometimes. We just want someone to tell us the shortcut to obedience. We're busy and don't have much time for messing around. We feel that we really should be able to manage obedience. We keep trying and failing. This book is not "obedience made easy". This book is a call to give ourselves to careful, patient, gospel-driven lives, where slowly we learn to joyfully obey God.

Honesty about my weakness (I can't), confession of my failure (I'm sorry), dependence on God's power (Please help), and only then do we jump to our feet (Let's go).

There are some waves coming. And they are real beauties. Let's learn to ride these waves.

Over to you
There are over 1,000 commands (waves) just in the New Testament. For the rest of this book, I've chosen eight that feel particularly impossible. Feel free to choose which to ride first.

4. Love God

I didn't choose it. I wasn't in control of it. I couldn't stop it. But it happened.

One moment I was cycling along the street and everything was fine. The next I was falling. I had lost control and was now hurtling through the air. Time slowed down. I didn't. Until I crunched into the tarmac.

I'm not a fan of falling. So it seems strange to me that the language of falling is so closely associated with the idea of love.

We fall in love.

I don't choose it. I'm not in control of it. I can't stop it. But it happens.

Elvis Presley summed this up well in in his iconic hit, "I can't help falling in love with you".

We have other ways of saying the same thing about love. We talk of being "swept off my feet" or of someone "stealing my heart" or of being "head over heels". Each of these conveys the same thing. Love is a powerful, irresistible, irrational force that cannot be controlled. I can't choose who I love.

Love is something that happens to me. Of course, I have some choice about whether I act on the feelings. I might feel love and choose to suppress it. Or I might be so overwhelmed by love that I seem to be powerless to stop it. But the fact remains that I can't help whether I fall in love or not. That's not under my control.

When the Bible talks of loving God, it doesn't mean that. It really doesn't.

Love is a command
When Jesus was asked about the greatest command, his answer was very clear.

> *"The most important one," answered Jesus, "is this: 'Hear, O Israel: the Lord our God, the Lord is one. Love the Lord your God with all your heart and with all your soul and with all your mind and with all your strength.'"*
> *(Mark 12 v 29-30)*

When we talk about obedience and commands, it starts here. The greatest command in all the world is that we should love God. At the risk of stating the obvious, it is a *command*. That means we are in the territory of obedience and disobedience rather than simply feelings and emotions. The Bible never talks of us "falling in love with God". Rather, it talks of us making the choice to obey or disobey.

When we say to God, "I love you", that's not primarily a statement about the emotional state of our heart. Rather, it declares a desire to obey God's greatest command.

I'm not saying that love for God is divorced from our emotions and feelings. Certainly not. For many people, there are times of intense emotion and experience in their relationship with God. But it would be a big mistake to imagine that experience is the sum total of what the Bible means when it talks about loving God. The foundation of loving God rests on the simple question of obedience. Whether we feel overwhelmed by emotion or as dry as a desert makes no difference to the question of whether we obey the command to love God.

When it comes to loving God, obedience comes first.

What is love?
Jesus didn't pluck the greatest commandment out of nowhere. He was quoting the Old Testament. God first gave this command to Israel back in Deuteronomy 6. Israel were God's chosen, rescued, precious people, and they were commanded to love God. But what does that really mean? I don't think God was expecting a whole selection of gushy love songs as people were swept off their feet in great emotional experiences. No—it was far simpler than that.

To love God means that you don't love other gods.

You pledge your allegiance, your heart, your life, your resources, everything you have to God. You abandon all other gods.

On the day I got married, I promised to love my wife. A key part of what that means was explained when I said, "forsaking all others". On that day I made a staggeringly big choice. I said NO to every other woman in the whole world (not that there was a very long queue of women weeping outside the ceremony—but you get the point).

That is what God is commanding his people. He spells out the negative of the command in the first of the Ten Commandments:

You shall have no other gods before me.

(Exodus 20 v 3)

You love God by forsaking all others.

As Israel entered the land God had promised them, there were lots of other gods around. They were confronted with other lovers who wanted their worship. This is what the Bible means by idolatry. It is when we give the love and worship that God deserves to anyone or anything that is not God. It is when we put anything in the place that God alone deserves.

The tragedy is that, rather than decide to love God in obedience to his command, God's people were seduced and fell in love with the gods of the nations. I have chosen the language here carefully. At the heart of idolatry is a deception that seeks to capture our affections. This is one of the big differences between God and the idols.

God loves us and commands our love. The false gods seduce us and steal our hearts.

Israel disobeyed God and chose to love idols. It ultimately led to their downfall. It's fascinating that idolatry is the BIG sin that Israel returned to again and again. This makes it very clear that disobedience is not about breaking a few rules—but about *who your heart loves*.

This isn't just about Israel. There are still plenty of other gods around ready to seduce us and steal our hearts. We need to wake up to the reality of our hearts and hear God's command to love him.

A young man
The book of Proverbs powerfully pictures this for us. Our hearts by nature will "fall in love" with all sorts of things. We will find ourselves powerfully captivated, entranced and swept off our feet by sin.

Read this story of a young man. Watch how he falls.

At the window of my house
    I looked down through the lattice.
I saw among the simple,
    I noticed among the young men,
    a youth who had no sense.

He was going down the street near her corner,
    walking along in the direction of her house
at twilight, as the day was fading,
    as the dark of night set in.

Then out came a woman to meet him,
    dressed like a prostitute and with crafty intent.
(She is unruly and defiant,
    her feet never stay at home;
now in the street, now in the squares,
    at every corner she lurks.)
She took hold of him and kissed him
    and with a brazen face she said:

"Today I fulfilled my vows,
    and I have food from my fellowship offering at home.
So I came out to meet you;
    I looked for you and have found you!
I have covered my bed
    with coloured linens from Egypt.
I have perfumed my bed
    with myrrh, aloes and cinnamon.
Come, let's drink deeply of love till morning;
    let's enjoy ourselves with love!
My husband is not at home;
    he has gone on a long journey.
He took his purse filled with money
    and will not be home till full moon."

With persuasive words she led him astray;
    she seduced him with her smooth talk.

All at once he followed her
  like an ox going to the slaughter,
like a deer stepping into a noose
  till an arrow pierces his liver,
like a bird darting into a snare,
  little knowing it will cost him his life.

                                    (Proverbs 7 v 6-23)

Can you imagine interviewing this young man after this night?

What on earth happened to you?

I don't know. I just couldn't help it. I was just minding my own business when she came and grabbed me. She said that it would be ok. She said that no one would know.

Why didn't you just go home?

I couldn't. It was so powerful. She was so beautiful. What was I supposed to do?

This young man experienced a classic case of falling. *I didn't choose it. I wasn't in control of it. I couldn't stop it.* But it happened.

Look at the tactics of sinful folly. The woman here is actively seeking people out. She is blatant and ready to pounce. She appeals to pleasure. She speaks words that seduce. The young man falls. He had no chance.

Just a victim?

But hold on one second. There's more going on. He was ensnared, seduced and led astray into her trap. But that doesn't make him a victim here. In one sense, he was not choosing this path—in another sense, he absolutely made the choice. He chose to walk on the street where she lives. He chose to go there just as the day was ending and night was falling. He chose to go near. And then he fell.

Imagine I choose to ride my bike within two inches of the edge of a cliff. And then I fall. I might still say that I didn't choose it, I'm not in control of it, and I can't stop it. But you would rightly point out that I did choose where I took my bike. That is my folly—especially if I passed numerous signs warning me of the dangers of the cliff that I was approaching.

Idols are powerful and seductive. We fall in love. But we also make the choice to be there. We make the choice to not love God. That is our folly. The command to love God is part of the way God protects us from the irresistible power of false gods.

We are back at the "can't obey, won't obey" dilemma (see pages 43-44).

Have you experienced something like this?

You find yourself "falling in love" with something that takes a hold of your heart. Rather than obeying the command to love God, you follow your heart and love something else.

"Let's not think that it's ok to try to keep loving God but to add some idol-worship on the side. That would be like me claiming that I love my wife but also having a mistress. My wife would never accept that— and neither will the Lord."

_____

IMPOSSIBLE
COMMANDS

Our hearts are powerfully drawn to "fall in love" with many things. Power is seductive and can captivate us. Sexual pleasure seduces and offers to satisfy us. Jesus talks about the "deceitfulness of wealth" (Mark 4 v 18-19). The list could go on. There are many lovers that come to us offering the world.

It's when we fail to obey the command to love God that we become vulnerable to the seductions of all sorts of other gods.

So what are we supposed to do with this command to love God? The answer is not to try harder. Instead, let's take the four steps we thought about in chapter 3 and apply them carefully to this command.

The Four Steps
I can't

God has given us this clear command to love him with all our heart, soul, strength and mind. He has spelled that out by warning us against having any other gods before him. He is very clear in demanding our undivided love. That is his command.

But that is impossible.

The sort of love that God is talking about here is far beyond us. We do not have the power to obey this command. In fact, we find the exact opposite. Rather than loving God, we are seduced by other gods.

Rather than being captivated by the Creator God who loves us, we chase after other things that ensnare us with their offers of satisfaction. And let's not think that it's ok to try and do both—to keep loving God but to add some idol-worship on the side. That would be like me claiming that I love my wife but also having a mistress. My wife would never accept that—and neither will the Lord.

We are very naive if we think that we don't have a problem in this area. Think of the young man in Proverbs. Where are you tempted to go? What are you tempted to do? What is it that your heart could easily fall in love with? Do you know where the danger lies for you? Try and be specific. What are the things that are most attractive to you? Be honest about how powerful they are.

Once we begin to walk down that road, we quickly lose control and find ourselves falling. How many times have you found yourself ensnared and powerless?

Sometimes we imagine that we're strong enough to love God in our own strength. We imagine that we'll never let him down. We'll always love him. We would never be seduced by sin and turn away from God. We make great claims of undying devotion—and in the moment we genuinely mean it. But that sort of self-confidence is to completely fail to see the danger. We need to be more real. We need to be more honest. We can't love God. We will be snared by other lovers.

And that should lead us to Step Two...

I'm sorry
Just because I can't love God with all my heart, soul, mind and strength does not mean that I'm not guilty.

As we get honest about our powerlessness in the face of idols, we need to confess our part in that. God is supremely good. He has saved us and chosen us to be his precious people. Yet rather than love him, we are so quick to turn away. That's shocking. It shows just how distorted our hearts really are.

We need to admit our guilt in loving other gods. It probably won't be the statues and images that we find people turning to in the Bible. It's much more likely to be our love of comfort, or pleasure, or power, or success, or possessions. We fall in love with these things. They seduce us and steal our hearts away from God.

We need to feel our guilt in loving other gods. We need to not make excuses for our failure. To not try and cover up. This is why Jesus had to die. He died because we do not love God. He died for all the times we have been seduced by idols. He died for all the times we have been unfaithful to God. He has paid for all of that failure.

Only when you feel the weight of failure, can you taste the sweetness of forgiveness. We deserve to be rejected and punished by God for ever. Yet, instead, he sent Jesus to win us back to himself.

God loves you—despite your failure, despite your divided heart. He loves you and has forgiven you.

Take hold of that forgiveness by faith. As you confess your sin, you must hear his promise that you are forgiven.

But it doesn't end there. As we confess, we find hope that this command will become something we can obey.

Please help

We are absolutely powerless in the face of idols, but God is not. God's command once stood against us and revealed our failure. But when we admit our sin and turn to Jesus, we become God's precious child. Now the command to love him is a command that comes from our loving heavenly Father.

Remember that God's commands come accompanied with the power to do what is commanded. So when he commands us to love him, he will enable our obedience. Sometimes that's hard to believe. Sometimes we look at our hearts—and our love for God seems so small, and our love for other things seems overwhelmingly powerful.

We find it hard to imagine that this could ever change. But God is more powerful than your love for other things. He really can begin to change you.

You need to lift your eyes and have this sort of confidence. Here are some specific things you could pray:

Heavenly Father, please help me to see the false promises that the idols make and the beautiful truth we find in Jesus. Help me to see that I'm stepping into a trap and that this road leads to the grave. Please will you change what my heart loves. Please will your Holy Spirit help me to know the freedom that is found in loving you. Thank you that you promise to give me the power to change, and I ask you for that power now. Help me not to go near those places where I know temptation lies. Help me to get rid of those things that make me stumble again and again. Help me to forsake all others and have a heart devoted to you.

Come like a child running to their Father. Come urgently. Come persistently.

What a beautiful and magnificent thing that is. The more clearly we see our Father, the more we will love him.

Let's go
Now (and only now) we prepare ourselves to take action. You joyfully and confidently make the decision to love God. God is very clear what you're supposed to do with idols. In the Old Testament Israel was told:

This is what you are to do to them: break down their altars, smash their sacred stones, cut down their Asherah poles and burn their idols in the fire.
(Deuteronomy 7 v 5)

In the New Testament you find similar kinds of language against idolatry. For example:

Put to death, therefore, whatever belongs to your earthly nature: sexual immorality, impurity, lust, evil desires and greed, which is idolatry.
(Colossians 3 v 5)

At first sight, you might think that smashing things and "putting to death" all sounds a bit negative. Don't be fooled. This sort of action is life-giving and glorious. Imagine a prisoner locked up with heavy chains. As you smash those chains, you set them free. As you break down the walls of the prison cell, you let light flood in and open the way to new life. That is the sort of smashing we are talking about.

As you make the decision to love God, you are not sacrificing any hope of a happy life. You are embracing the life that you were made for and the Father who loves you.

So let's be practical. What specific changes could you make to show a desire to love God above all else? What do you need to change/remove/adjust/rethink? Pray for God's help and then make the changes: real choices, real action, real changes driven by real love.

It will be a lifetime of battle, but there is joy here. Deep and lasting joy.

> *The most important [command] ... is this: "Hear, O Israel: the Lord our God, the Lord is one. Love the Lord your God with all your heart and with all your soul and with all your mind and with all your strength."*
> *(Mark 12 v 29-30)*

5. Rejoice in the Lord (always)

I thought the t-shirt was a great idea. But it wasn't. I thought it would brighten things up and spread a little joy and happiness. But it didn't. Looking back, I should have spotted the problem much sooner. But I couldn't see the danger.

It sounds innocent enough. It was just a blue t-shirt with the words "Mr Happy" on the front. It also had an enormous, yellow, smiling cartoon character beaming out to the world.

The problems started when people noticed a serious disconnection between my face and my t-shirt. I don't live my life in a state of euphoric happiness. There are some days when I feel a bit miserable, and other days when I feel decidedly grumpy. In any other t-shirt, my slightly-less-than-happy days might have passed without comment. But not in my Mr Happy t-shirt. For some reason people took my t-shirt as permission to point out to me that I didn't look very happy.

As you can imagine, that didn't improve my happiness levels. Strangers would comment about the state of my happiness as I walked down the street. And if I ever said anything that wasn't super-optimistic and positive, people would immediately come back with, "Well, someone isn't very Mr Happy today".

The t-shirt ended up in the bin.

Disconnection

I think many Christians have a similar experience as they follow Jesus. There is a disconnection between what we say we believe and our experience. We suspect that being a Christian is supposed to be a joyful thing, and we regularly hear in church that Christians are meant to rejoice, but the reality is often far from that.

I grew up during the 80's, and one of the songs we used to sing over and over (and over) in our youth group had the line:

My joy just keeps on growing.

As we sang that song, it was hard not to feel something of a Mr-Happy-t-shirt moment. There often a disconnection between my words and my face. It just wasn't my experience that my joy kept growing. I did sometimes feel joyful—but more often than not I didn't. What was I supposed to do with this song?

Another song we used to sing had the line:

When the world has seen the light
They will dance with joy like we're dancing now.

It bothered me slightly, looking round at us all standing very still with our hands in our pockets. I remember thinking that we weren't really setting a very high bar for joy. If the world had popped their heads in to take a peek at what Christian joy looks like in action, they would not have been blown away.

All of that set me wondering: what does joy actually look like? How would you spot it? And how do you get anywhere near it?

That's what we're exploring in this chapter. We need to let God teach us what it really means to be joyful. We might find that we've got this wrong. We're in danger of placing joy in the wrong category and therefore settling for something less than God's great vision for our joy. It starts by recognising that joy is not primarily an experience to pursue, but rather, it is one of God's "impossible commands" that we obey by faith.

Commanded

In a number of places the Bible commands us to be joyful. As we look at a few examples, read them slowly and carefully, looking out for the language of command that is used.

The first example comes from the Old Testament law—the book of Leviticus no less. I realise this is not the first place we might turn to in order to learn about joy. We may be tempted to write off the whole of God's law as rather sombre and restrictive. But here's the surprise: *joy was built into God's law.* God's people were commanded to set aside time for rejoicing.

Here are instructions for one of their annual festivals:

> *On the first day you are to take branches from luxuriant trees—from palms, willows and other leafy trees— and rejoice before the LORD your God for seven days.*
>
> *(Leviticus 23 v 40)*

God is serious about joy. He knew that his people had a tendency towards joylessness, and so he commanded that they took time to intentionally and deliberately rejoice. That has got to make us stop and think about what joy really means. Can joy be turned on and off? How can you command a nation to feel joy? Seven days of joy? Is that even possible?

Here is a more general command from the psalms, showing that joy was to be a distinctive mark of God's righteous people:

> *Sing joyfully to the LORD, you righteous;*
> *   it is fitting for the upright to praise him.*
> *Praise the LORD with the harp;*
> *   make music to him on the ten-stringed lyre.*
> *Sing to him a new song;*
> *   play skilfully, and shout for joy.*
>
> *(Psalm 33 v 1-3)*

This is not just for one week of the year but is a general attitude of heart that is oriented in an outwardly joyful direction. The language here is about exuberant, noisy, skilfully expressed joy.

You see this in the New Testament too. The commands to be joyful keep on coming.

> *Be joyful in hope, patient in affliction, faithful in*
> *prayer.* (Romans 12 v 12)

> *Rejoice in the Lord always. I will say it again: rejoice!*
> (Philippians 4 v 4)

> *Rejoice always, pray continually, give thanks in all*
> *circumstances; for this is God's will for you in Christ*
> *Jesus.* (1 Thessalonians 5 v 16-18)

Even in the face of tough circumstances, the Bible commands us to be joyful:

> *Consider it pure joy, my brothers and sisters, whenever*
> *you face trials of many kinds, because you know that*
> *the testing of your faith produces perseverance.*
> (James 1 v 2-3)

These commands are not everything the Bible says about joy. There are plenty of other examples where rejoicing is a glorious and emotional response to what people have received from God. But I've highlighted the commands above to help us to get clear that rejoicing is part of our *obedience* rather than just our *experience*.

More than feelings

We often place joy in a bucket labelled "Feelings". It becomes an elusive experience that we try to capture. Sometimes we feel it—we are moved and thrilled and have a great emotional high—but then it seems to go again. And so the search continues. Maybe we try different forms of worship, different music, different traditions, or different preachers, trying to feel something.

It's like trying to reach a ball that's bobbing just out of reach on a lake. We reach for it and we just about touch it, but then it moves away again. Rather than becoming increasingly joyful, we often find ourselves increasingly dissatisfied with our everyday lives and our everyday churches.

But biblical joy is not an experience that we try to manufacture with the right atmosphere.

Psalm 33 places it in a bucket labelled "Action". The people of God are not being told to feel joy; they are being commanded to sing joyfully. This is a radical redefinition of joy. Joy is something that you *do* before it is something that you *feel*. Getting things in their right order matters enormously.

Worldly joy is driven by feelings. I cannot control it. Something happens in my life that makes me feel good, and so I rejoice. The feeling of joy overflows into the action of rejoicing. Our football team scores, and so we sing. We win a competition, so we celebrate and rejoice.

"Joy is something that you *do* before it is something that you *feel*."

IMPOSSIBLE
COMMANDS

Worldly happiness is a temporary state that is brought about by circumstances. When things go well, I rejoice. But I know that the vacation will end, or my career will go wrong, or my health will fail, and then my joy will be gone. So we get caught up in an endless cycle of trying to chase the things that we think will make us feel joy.

Biblical joy is different. In fact, it's the other way round. Joyful praise comes first as an act of obedience whether or not I feel it. It is not grounded in my ever-changing circumstances but in the unchanging nature of God.

(By the way, don't hear me say that joy has nothing to do with feelings—we will get to that later—but it must start here.)

Optional joy?

Here is another danger with our normal view of joy. We place joy in a bucket labelled "Optional Extra". It is a bonus but non-essential component to being a Christian. Nice to have but you can live without it. Like a hot tub in the garden.

But Psalm 33 places joy in a bucket labelled "Essential Obedience". The writer of the psalm talks about it being fitting and right, and absolutely what God's righteous people will do (v 1). Joyful praise is not just a nice thing but a right thing. Which means that not rejoicing becomes a wrong thing. When we don't rejoice in God, we are sinning.

That last sentence is pretty strong and maybe stirs up some concern in you. Perhaps you're starting to think it is entirely unreasonable to live life in a constant sense of joy.

Except that Paul says in Philippians, "Rejoice in the Lord *always*" (Philippians 4 v 4).

If you're beginning to feel that this is too hard, then you're right. If you're beginning to think to yourself, "I can't joyfully praise God all the time—that's impossible", then that's great. You're already into Step One of joyful obedience. As we work out our four steps in relation to this command, we are going to see how joy can become increasingly part of our obedience. But first, let's find out what Jesus had to say about joy...

Jesus wants you to be joyful

It was the night before Jesus would die on the cross. In John 17, he is praying to his Father. We get a fascinating glimpse into the thoughts and priorities that fill his mind as he prepares for the most overwhelming ordeal any human being has ever experienced. What do we find?

First, Jesus is concerned for his Father's glory. Then, he is concerned for his disciples. They are going to be in great danger, and so he prays for their protection. It's going to be intensely hard for those disciples to live in a world that hates them. But Jesus has a bigger ambition for them than simply survival. Look at the words he prays:

> *I am coming to you now, but I say these things while*
> *I am still in the world, so that they may have the full*
> *measure of my joy within them.*   *(John 17 v 13)*

On the night before he died, Jesus was concerned that his disciples would know joy. And not just a little joy, but the full measure of joy that he has for them.

Jesus wants his disciples to be joyful.

To pursue joy is not a selfish endeavour. It is to pursue what Jesus died for. He died for our joy—for yours and for mine. He died and rose again that we might know the deepest and richest joy imaginable.

We often make the mistake of thinking that sin will bring us joy, and God will spoil our joy. It is an enormous lie. To choose to reject God and live for ourselves and our own pleasure does not lead to everlasting joy. It leads to temporary, weak and, ultimately, fading joy.

Jesus went to the cross to die because we have pursued joy in the wrong places. Jesus died because he wants you to discover the joy you were created for in relationship with God the Father.

Jesus wants you to be joyful. Eternally joyful. But that is going to take obedience. And that is going to need faith.

A case study
Habakkuk was a prophet who did not have much to be happy about. He lived around 600 years before the birth

of Christ, at a time when things were terrible all around him. God's people were a mess; there was injustice and evil. And God was doing nothing about it.

Habakkuk was not joyful. So he cried out to God for answers.

God's answer made things worse. He told Habakkuk that he was going to send the Babylonians to punish Israel. This did not help.

But Habakkuk kept waiting and calling on God for answers.

Then God spoke. He spoke of "the end" (Habakkuk 2 v 3). He spoke of the day when all wickedness would be punished. He spoke of the day when "the earth will be filled with the knowledge of the glory of the LORD as the waters cover the sea" (Habakkuk 2 v 14).

And Habakkuk believed God's word. Listen to his testimony at the end of the book.

Though the fig-tree does not bud
  and there are no grapes on the vines,
though the olive crop fails
  and the fields produce no food,
though there are no sheep in the sheepfold
  and no cattle in the stalls,
yet I will rejoice in the LORD,
  I will be joyful in God my Saviour.

(Habakkuk 3 v 17-18)

The circumstances have not changed at all. There is still no good stuff around. But Habakkuk is trusting God's word, and he makes the decision to rejoice.

Listen to it. This is DEFIANT JOY. Despite everything—yet I will rejoice.

This is not passive worldly joy that comes along when things are good. This is active, defiant, obedient joy.

Habakkuk has heard God's word, and he makes the decision to rejoice.

The Four Steps
Let's take all of that and work it through using the four steps we have been exploring.

I can't
It is ok to be honest with God about how you are feeling. Habakkuk was honest. We don't have to pretend to be feeling something that we aren't. How many times have you stood in church, and the songs have started—and you just can't be bothered to sing. You don't feel even a flicker of anything.

It's tempting when that happens to shrug our shoulders and say, "Oh well, I just don't feel it today. I'll stand here quietly until I can sit down again." Or perhaps we make a half-hearted effort to sing.

How about a different approach? How about being honest with God?

"Lord, I can't rejoice today. I don't feel excited about you. I don't have any desire to praise you for your character or for your kindness towards me. I can't do it."

Do you ever speak to God like that? It's liberating to be honest with God. He knows the truth anyway. We don't need to put on an act and pretend that everything is fine.

But you don't stop there. That honesty leads to confession.

I'm sorry
Our lack of joy is a symptom that something is wrong. So we need to confess it.

"I confess that my lack of joy is sinful. It is wrong and shows that sin is deeply rooted in my heart. Lord, you are always good and always worthy of praise. You have not changed; you never change. You gave your Son for me. Please forgive me for my cold and hard heart. Please forgive me that I would be more joyful about the temporary things of this world rather than you."

You could pray like this as you stand in church not wanting to sing. Or as you struggle to open your Bible in the morning. Or as you find your heart far more excited about a new house than about Jesus.

Please help
Now is the point that you look away from yourself and ask God for help. "Please give me joy." If the Father

commands you to be joyful, then you can be sure that his word will come with all the power necessary to obey. The Lord Jesus died for your joy. The Holy Spirit has been given to you so that you might be joyful. Joy is one segment of the fruit of the Spirit that he is committed to growing in every Christian's life (Galatians 5 v 22-23). This is terrific news. Joy is not something that we have the responsibility to generate by our own willpower. It is produced as God works in us.

We don't have to attend a great conference, or put on the right music, or pursue a new experience. We simply have to ask.

Have you asked God to give you joy?

Then don't just stand there and wait to be zapped. Do something.

Let's go
Don't wait to feel it. Don't wait for circumstances to change. Follow the example of Habakkuk in his defiant joy: *Despite everything, I will rejoice in God.* Then get on with rejoicing, even if the feelings don't come.

Here are a couple of practical suggestions for ways to defiantly praise God. I'm sure you can think of more.

Don't take this the wrong way, but I want to encourage you to sing louder. If you are in church and don't feel joy, once you have confessed it and asked God for help, then open your mouth and obey Psalm 33. The colder my heart feels, the louder I try to sing. This is the defiance of joy. I will not let my cold heart set the agenda for my life today. Often, as I begin to obey, I then experience the feelings of joy. But even when I don't, it is right and good to obey God. That is faith in action.

Use the psalms. When you don't want to rejoice, you can use the words that God has given for us to praise him. Read a psalm. (Psalms 96 and 98 would be good places to start.) I suggest you do it out loud. You could try to memorise a psalm, and that way you can rejoice in God as you walk down the street. There is a battle for joy. We have a part to play as we walk in obedience.

We will often feel the Mr Happy disconnection. We will often find that our experience doesn't match what we know we ought to feel. But don't ditch the t-shirt. Don't give up on joy and settle for a mediocre, joyless Christianity. That's not what Jesus wants for you. He commands us to rejoice, and he promises the power to make it happen.

Rejoice in the Lord always. I will say it again: rejoice!
(Philippians 4 v 4)

6. Be perfect

In fairness, the wallpaper wasn't exactly straight. There were a few bubbles. And some (smallish) rips. These were made slightly more obvious because it was black wallpaper (interesting choice, I know, but it was very cheap) and a white wall behind. But a little dab of black permanent marker pen, and I was fairly happy with the result. I comforted myself with the thought: *Oh well, no one is perfect.*

It's funny how often that little thought is a comfort to us. It excuses all sorts of minor indiscretions and bumps and slip-ups—and some major ones as well.

The idea of perfection threatens us because it shows us up. Imperfection comforts us because it reassures us that we are ok.

No parent would ever expect perfection from their child. No teacher would ever expect it from their students. After all, everyone knows that no one is perfect.

Which is why our next command is so uncomfortable.

In Matthew's Gospel, as part of the teaching known as the Sermon on the Mount, Jesus says:

> *Be perfect, therefore, as your heavenly Father is perfect.*
> *(Matthew 5 v 48)*

A little unreasonable?

I looked up the Greek word for "perfect"—just to make sure. It has the idea of being finished, complete, not lacking anything. And just to be clear, the completeness Jesus has in view is that of God himself. Basically, it really does mean perfect. There's no way to get round it.

Perfect is not a relative term. We had a long-running dispute in our home about whether something could be "almost perfect". I would often use the phrase and would instantly be told that something is either perfect or it's not. You can't be *almost* perfect. I realise that there are bigger things to worry about, so please don't feel the need to take sides, but it does make a point. Strictly speaking, perfection is absolute.

Most of us tend to approach life with a far more relative attitude. I try my best, and as long as I'm not too bad, I'm relatively satisfied. Jesus doesn't seem to share that sentiment for his followers. He is far more ambitious. His command really is, "Be perfect".

Let's be honest, it sounds pretty unreasonable. Surely he can't be serious. It feels pretty crushing.

It would be easy to shake our heads and write this off as impossible.

Oh, wait a second... Hopefully that thought is familiar to us by now. Yes, *all* of God's commands are impossible. This is just another one. So, if we can get past the shock, perhaps this command might become exciting and hope-filled for us.

That's something to look forward to, but first up, we need to understand a bit of background to Jesus' command.

Back to Moses

When Jesus said this 2000 years ago, he was picking up on a command that his Jewish audience would have been very familiar with. Here's something very similar on the lips of Moses. He is told by God to...

> *Speak to the entire assembly of Israel and say to them:*
> *"Be holy because I, the LORD your God, am holy."*
> > *(Leviticus 19 v 2)*

Both commands are structured in a remarkably similar way.

> *Be perfect, therefore, as your heavenly Father is perfect.*
> > *(Matthew 5 v 48)*

> *Be holy because I, the LORD your God, am holy.*
> > *(Leviticus 19 v 2)*

Here is the basic ethical demand of the Old Testament law. It starts with the character of our fantastic God. He is holy. From there the command flows outwards towards his people. In order to understand the command, it has to start with God.

So come with me as we explore a little of the wonderful holiness of God. It will be a few paragraphs before we get back to the command, but it will be well worth the detour...

The holiness of God

Holiness is one of God's essential attributes. It's not simply that God possesses holiness. It's not just that God's actions are holy. It's not merely that God loves holiness. No—it defines what God is. He is holy. Holiness is who God is.

It's not easy to pin down a definition of holiness, but that shouldn't stop us trying. Perhaps you begin to grasp a sense of it when you think of Moses' first ever encounter with God. In Exodus chapter 3, Moses sees a bush that is on fire but does not burn up. He approaches the bush to look more closely. Then God says to him:

> *Do not come any closer ... Take off your sandals, for the place where you are standing is holy ground.*
>
> *(Exodus 3 v 5)*

Holiness means that Moses cannot come close. This bit of ground is different. It's not like any other bit of ground, so you must take off your sandals. You begin to see that there is something awesome, something unapproachable, something utterly "other" when God comes near.

Over and over again in the Old Testament you see a similar experience of God's holiness. When the people came to Mount Sinai—the mountain top where God has descended—they had to be kept at a distance. Moses said to God:

> *The people cannot come up Mount Sinai, because you*
> *yourself warned us, "Put limits around the mountain*
> *and set it apart as holy."*   *(Exodus 19 v 23)*

Do you see the same language again? This mountain is not like any other mountain. It is holy. It cannot simply be treated like a normal mountain. God's presence sanctifies (makes holy) the mountain, and that means that people can't come up. Only one man can go up—only the man that God has chosen. Holiness keeps people out.

Then it happens again when the people build a tent (known as the tabernacle) for God's presence. In the very centre of the tabernacle was the Most Holy Place. You could not just walk into that place. Only one man, once a year, following a very specific set of instructions, was allowed in. The message is pretty clear. The holiness of God is dangerous and serious. You don't mess around in this place.

Why all these restrictions? Why did the people have to keep their distance? It is because holiness and sin cannot mix. If something unholy came into contact with something holy, that was a very dangerous encounter and nearly always ended in death.

God's holiness is his absolute separation from anything impure. God is not like us—that is his holiness. There is nothing in him that spoils him. Nothing. God's holiness demands that sin is kept away.

So is holiness bad news or good news?

At this point, you could be forgiven for thinking that the idea of holiness is a pretty negative thing. It's fair to say that we don't often associate holiness with joy. It feels far more sombre and serious. We might even think that God's holiness means he wants nothing to do with us because we are definitely not pure and perfect in every way.

But to simply see holiness that way would be a big mistake. If God just wanted to remain separate from sin, then he could have stayed in heaven and washed his hands of any further part in the history of earth. If that was the expression of God's holiness, that really would be terrible news.

But, wonderfully, God's holiness doesn't do that.

He comes near. He appears in a burning bush; he descends to a mountain top; he dwells in a tent. His holiness keeps us away, and yet also he comes close to us. His holiness is terrifying and yet beautiful. God's holiness doesn't drive him to write off sinners as lost causes. Rather, it goes in completely the opposite direction. It is the holiness of

God that drives him to work to make a people for himself who can also be called holy.

A holy nation
In the Old Testament, God's people Israel were called a "holy nation". That should strike you as a remarkable thing after all we've seen. God alone is holy—it is his essential essence—and now a group of people are being called by the same word?

Remember the bush, the mountain and the tent. The bush was no ordinary bush. It was set apart; it was different. God's presence had made it holy.

So it was with God's people. They were no ordinary people. God had rescued them from slavery. He had chosen them; he had spoken to them; and crucially he had come down to live among them. So they were holy.

The Leviticus question
But how is that possible? How can the holy God live among sinful people? Surely that's impossible. May I suggest that you pause to feel the weight and significance of that question? Our Lord is totally, perfectly, awesomely holy. If we don't see the issue, we probably haven't grasped the holiness of God.

We can be in danger of treating sin very lightly. We know that God forgives us and loves us, and so we can be tempted to think sin is no big deal. But the holiness of God pushes us to stop for a moment and think. God is still absolutely holy, and therefore he cannot simply smile and tolerate sin.

This is such a big question in the Old Testament that there is a whole book of the Bible dedicated to answering it: the magnificent book of Leviticus! By the end of the book of Exodus, we see God living among his people in the tabernacle that they have made. Sounds great—but you can't escape the question, how is that *possible*?

There are really only two options. Either the people have to make themselves holy (not going to happen) or God needs to provide a way to make the people holy.

Leviticus explains with breathtaking power that God provides the way (Leviticus 16). It shows what is required for the holy God to live among unholy people.

He makes a way for their sin to be atoned for, dealt with, completely removed. Sin is transferred to an animal substitute. The animal is then sacrificed to pay the penalty sin deserves and to take it away (that is atonement). The people are then made holy.

Here is the key. They do not make themselves holy: God makes them holy. And only then does Moses issue the command (here we are back at the command again):

> *Be holy because I, the LORD your God, am holy.*
>
> *(Leviticus 19 v 2)*

The people are not being told to achieve holiness—God has provided that for them. They are already his holy

"Perfection is not a target we're aiming for; it's a gift we have received. Perfection is not the standard you have to hit to be accepted in God's family; it's the standard Jesus has met to welcome you in."

IMPOSSIBLE
COMMANDS

people. This is not about achieving holiness; this is about *living out who they truly are.*

God is holy.

He makes his people holy.

He then commands them to live out that holiness.

The Numbers problem

Unfortunately, in the next book of the Bible, Numbers (and from then onwards), the people do not live out this status. They become like all the other nations. They act as if they are not special, not different, not set apart.

The bush got it, but the people don't. They fail again and again. They want a king like the other nations. They want gods like the other nations. They want armies like the other nations.

They are supposed to be holy but they aren't. So God is rightly angry, and he punishes his people.

Clearly something more is required—and, wonderfully, something more is planned.

In Matthew 5 v 1, Jesus goes up a mountainside in Galilee (sounds a lot like Moses). But things are different with Jesus. In Moses' day, the people had to stay at the bottom, but here the people come up the mountain to listen (both Jesus' disciples and the crowds, Matthew 7 v 28). Here is a clue that Jesus is going to do more than Moses ever could.

Jesus teaches them and then issues the command:

> *Be perfect, therefore, as your heavenly Father is perfect.*
> *(Matthew 5 v 48)*

A perfect Father

Just as with Moses, Jesus' command is rooted in the character of God. The Lord is perfect. He hasn't changed since the days of Moses. He hasn't lowered his standards; he has not become more tolerant of sin; he is not making things easier. But Jesus calls God our "heavenly Father".

The same question arises: How can the perfect God call imperfect people to be his children? How can God do that without messing up his own perfection? We are right back in Leviticus territory.

It won't surprise you to know that the answer is just the same (but better!). God makes his children perfect. He makes them holy. Just as he did in Leviticus, God provides a way for imperfect people to be made perfect. But it is not now an animal sacrifice that stands in our place—it is the spotless, perfect, holy Son of God.

Jesus Christ died in our place. As we come to him, and admit our unholiness (all the ways we have failed) and look to him for help, that sin is transferred to him and he deals with it completely. As Jesus died on the cross, God's anger was satisfied and our sin was removed, and now we can be his children.

The perfection and holiness of God does not cause him to stand at a distance and shake his head. It drives him to come so close in order that he can make us holy and take us as his children.

Then, and only then, does he issue the command. Your heavenly Father is perfect. If you have put your trust in Jesus, God has accepted you, cleansed you, purified you, made you perfect. So now live it out.

Perfection is not a target we're aiming for; it's a gift we have received. Perfection is not the standard you have to hit to be accepted in God's family; it's the standard Jesus has met to welcome you in.

A lifetime

So perfection is really good news. It is what God is like, and he is beautiful. It is the gift God has given us as he welcomes us into his family. And all of that means that perfection now becomes the privilege we pursue.

We live out what God has given us—not in fear but with joy.

This was the apostle Paul's great vision for the church. He preached the beautiful gospel of Jesus with a very clear aim.

> *He is the one we proclaim, admonishing and teaching everyone with all wisdom, so that we may present everyone fully mature* [the same word as "perfect"] *in Christ.* *(Colossians 1 v 28)*

We tend to settle for something far less than the plans God has for us. We love the message of forgiveness and of sin being dealt with completely—but we don't always allow that to overflow into an urgent and passionate desire for perfection.

The people in the Old Testament failed to live as God's holy people. They did not have the power to live it out. So what hope have we got of doing any better? Won't we just fail too?

The coming of Jesus has also brought one other massive change. In order that we might live as his holy people, he has given us his Holy Spirit. The clue is in the name. The Holy Spirit lives in us, and it is as we walk in step with him that we find the power to live this new life.

It is impossible for us—but not with God. Everything is possible with him (Luke 18 v 27).

When we understand who we are as God's precious children, it changes everything. When we understand that God has given us his Holy Spirit to enable us to change, it changes everything. The perfection of God becomes a beautiful reality that can inspire us to pursue more. There is hope and joy here as we see what God has planned for us.

Let me be clear that the Bible says that we will not achieve perfection in this life. We will fail. We will still sin. But that is not to define us anymore. On the days when we mess up, we confess that sin and find Jesus to be the one who deals with it completely. Then we go again. Little by little we make progress; bit by bit we win victories over sin. It's a painful struggle, but we don't stop fighting. And one day, Jesus will return, and we will be made to be like him. On that day, perfection comes and the battle is over. But until that day, let perfection inspire you and encourage you and drive you on to be more and more like Jesus.

The Four Steps
I can't

Perfection is out of our reach. But it doesn't therefore mean that it should be off our radar. Jesus is not calling us to a "manageable" level of holiness. He is not asking us to try and do the best we can.

Neither are we supposed to spend our lives comparing ourselves to others and comforting ourselves with the thought that no one is perfect. That just leads to a tolerating of sin. It means we shrug our shoulders and get complacent. The vision that God has for you is so much better than that.

But it's not something you can achieve on your own.

Where are you aware of imperfections in your life? What are the ways in which you behave that you know aren't great but you tolerate?

Be honest with God about the fact that you cannot be perfect. Tell him about the big and little things that you really struggle with. Tell him how hard you find it and how tempted you are to give up even trying. Tell him the ways in which you have settled for "good enough". Look out for the ways that you are excusing sin.

I'm sorry

Now confess those things to him. God is not only bothered about the big sins. He doesn't have a level that he is hoping you might get to. 70% is not the pass mark.

Spend some time meditating on the sheer holiness and perfection of God. Don't compare yourself to people around you—we can always find people who make us look good.

Rather, think about the holiness of God and confess your sin. We treat sin lightly when we fail to see God as he really is. When God is small, our failure is no big deal. But when we begin to see the absolute holiness of God, the thought of even the smallest sin will make us tremble. Confession doesn't start by looking inside and seeing what makes me feel bad. It starts by looking at God and seeing how desperately far short I fall.

But as you confess, remember what God has done. His holiness does not keep you out; his perfection does not drive you away. God has provided the way to make you perfect. Every single sin—the big and the small—has been placed on Jesus and dealt with completely.

You can stand in the holy presence of God as one of his holy and perfect children—without fear.

Only Jesus has lived the perfect life. Only Jesus can forgive our failures. Only Jesus can bring us hope.

Please help

All who have come to Jesus have already been made holy. That is your status and identity. You have been joined to Jesus, the Holy one, and you share his holiness. God has come to live in you by his Holy Spirit. What was temporarily true of the bush is now permanently true of you! So take some time to thank him.

Rather than defining your identity in terms of your failures, ask that God will help you to take hold of the new identity that is yours in Christ.

The command that Jesus gives to "be perfect" is not standing against you anymore. Where once God's command highlighted your failure, now it expresses God's purpose for your life. Allow this command to cause hope to rise within you: hope in the face of your failure—hope not in your power but in his.

Ask God to help you to joyfully pursue perfection, and to give you moments when you are truly perfect: a child in the likeness of your Father. God's Holy Spirit lives in us and makes us holy.

Take the struggles from Step One and ask specifically and carefully for God's power to make progress.

Let's go

It's worth repeating that we will not achieve perfection this side of heaven—but that shouldn't stop us going hard after it in God's power.

I find myself going back to the same old sins over and over again. When we get into a pattern, we can give up trying anymore. Perhaps this chapter will reawaken within us a desire to make progress. Perhaps the reality of God's perfect holiness will shake us out of complacency and help us to passionately pursue perfection.

In order for change to happen, we need to make some changes. What are the practical steps that will help you make progress? Don't be daunted by perfection—be inspired to make progress today.

And since perfection is the goal, a whole lifetime of joyful obedience lies ahead. Then one glorious day, Jesus will return—and the battle will be over and we will be perfect for ever.

Be perfect, therefore, as your heavenly Father is perfect.
(Matthew 5 v 48)

7. Don't be afraid

My editor is scared of spiders. So scared that she can never put a glass over one to catch it. Instead, she has to use a large mixing bowl. And once—because the eight-legged beast looked worryingly strong—she then weighed the bowl down with a heavy book until someone could come and rescue her. Yes, really.

We all feel afraid sometimes. We all get overwhelmed. It's a very normal human experience. But in the face of that fear, God says, "Don't be afraid". How do we even begin to obey that command?

First, let's think about fear. I find I experience fear when I realise that the resources I have do not match the situation that I'm facing.

Do you remember playing on a seesaw? It's great fun when you have a friend about the same size as you. You bounce up and down, and all is well. But it's a totally different game when a grown-up is on one end and a three-year-old at the other. The toddler does not have the resources to match the bulk of the adult. They are left stranded in mid-air with their legs flailing around. There is nothing they can do; they are completely at the mercy of the far heavier partner.

On a seesaw that might be fun, but when that happens in real life, it can be terrifying. Sometimes, a situation lands on one end of our seesaw, and we have nowhere near the resources needed to cope. It's far too big for us, and we're left stranded in mid-air desperately trying to find some way to get control. Our legs are waving around but we are nowhere near the ground. We just don't have power. Our efforts are futile—and so we get afraid.

The resources we have are no match for the situation we face. Have you ever felt like that?

Fear is personal
What are *you* scared of?

Our fears are quite personal to ourselves. It might be a serious illness or the death of a loved one, the loss of a job or shortage of money. Some of us fear failing, or how others will respond when we do. Others worry about seemingly smaller things, and then the fear is compounded by the additional fear of being mocked for a fear someone else never feels.

Some of us, thankfully, are rarely afraid; for others it's a daily struggle.

But whether our fears are big or small, rare or regular, the Lord invites us to bring them to him. He never mocks us for being afraid; but neither will he leave us like that. He calls us to come to him with our fears, whatever they are.

Beyond our ability

The things that frighten us aren't just the actual situations we face—sometimes it is the things that we think *might* happen that terrify us. We feel as if we're just about balancing the seesaw, but at any moment something big is going to land that will send us over the edge. We fear what *might* happen.

The apostle Paul writes about such things. Look at the language he uses in 2 Corinthians:

> *We were under great pressure, far beyond our ability to endure, so that we despaired of life itself.*
>
> *(2 Corinthians 1 v 8)*

Does that sound familiar to you? The pressure that was pushing down on Paul was so great that he was completely out of control. We all face these "beyond-our-ability" situations some of the time—when we know that we don't have what is needed.

Believe in yourself

We're not helped by the relentless message that we just need to "believe in ourselves". It comes from athletes, pop stars, self-help books, Disney movies and more.

They keep repeating the same basic message: there is a hero within you; there is a power within you; look within and unlock the power that you possess.

We hear this message and believe that we're supposed to be able to do anything, but then we find that situations come along that we do not have the power to deal with. That's when we get scared.

We have limited resources. Despite what our culture says, there are many situations that we face that are far beyond our ability. This is not giving up (we will get to a better way in a moment)—this is just being honest. And admitting our weakness is a great relief.

We don't have to pretend that we are in control; we don't have to pretend that we are coping. It's ok to admit that we feel like a three-year-old who is completely out of control and powerless to do anything about it.

A heavier solution
The Bible never minimises our fears. Over and over again we meet godly characters who experience fear. People like Abraham, Moses, Joshua, Esther, Gideon, David or Mary—in fact it's fairly hard to find a Bible character who didn't experience fear.

This is so important for us to realise. God does not view our fears as irrational or ridiculous, not even the "little" ones. He never suggests that we should just pull ourselves together. He never says that we are being silly.

Instead, he gives us a Bible that is full of people who were scared—all sorts of people facing all sorts of situations that were far, far beyond them. Fears are very real.

But neither does God let these fears have the last word.

The last word belongs to the Lord, and that word is always "Do not be afraid". It's God's standard response to our fears and is repeated over and over again in the pages of the Bible:

> *That night the* LORD *appeared to him and said, "I am the God of your father Abraham.* **Do not be afraid**, *for I am with you..."* (Genesis 26 v 24)

> *Moses answered the people, "***Do not be afraid**. *Stand firm and you will see the deliverance the* LORD *will bring you today."* (Exodus 14 v 13)

> **Do not be afraid**; *do not be discouraged, for the* LORD *your God will be with you wherever you go.*
> (Joshua 1 v 9)

> *But the angel said to her, "***Do not be afraid**, *Mary, you have found favour with God."* (Luke 1 v 30)

> *[Jesus said,] "Peace I leave with you; my peace I give you. I do not give to you as the world gives. Do not let your hearts be troubled and* **do not be afraid**."
> (John 14 v 27)

Once again, please notice that this is a command, not a suggestion or a motivational slogan. God is commanding his people not to be afraid.

Nice... but how?

How can God say that? How is it possible to not be afraid when life is so obviously beyond our ability?

The answer is pretty simple to understand (far more difficult to implement). Although there are many things that are beyond our ability, there is nothing that is ever beyond *his* ability. There is no problem, or battle, that is heavier than God. When God gets on our end of the seesaw, we find the power we need to get our feet back on the ground.

When God commands us to not be afraid, he's not suggesting that there is nothing to fear and that we should stop being silly. He's also not suggesting that we have the power within us if only we could look within. No, he is commanding us to remember all the resources that are in him and to find our security there. His command "Don't be afraid" comes with the powerful promise "I will be with you" (e.g. Deuteronomy 20 v 1, 31 v 8; Joshua 1 v 9; Acts 18 v 9-10; Philippians 4 v 6-9).

This is what Paul discovered when he faced "beyond-our-ability" situations. Listen to what he says:

> But this happened that we might not rely on ourselves but on God, who raises the dead. He has delivered us from such a deadly peril, and he will deliver us again. On him we have set our hope that he will continue to deliver us, as you help us by your prayers.
>
> *(2 Corinthians 1 v 9-11)*

This is the opposite of Disney theology. Paul's fear and despair did not drive him towards himself. Instead, it drove him to a deeper reliance on God. Paul did not look within; he looked to the Lord.

God is heavier than anything we will face. God is heavier even than death itself. Paul describes God as the One who raises the dead. With God on our side we have nothing to fear.

That all sounds fine in theory, but what does it really mean to obey this command to not be afraid?

Fear as the solution to fear

You'll have to bear with me for a second, because this is going to sound slightly weird—but the answer from the Bible is that the solution to our fears is to replace them with a greater fear.

It always puzzled me as a child that the solution to measles was measles. Inject a small dose of measles, and the body will build a natural immunity. Well, the solution to our fear is fear. But in this case it's not a small dose that we need but a much greater dose than we have ever realised. Confused? Keep reading.

In Exodus we read about a fascinating moment when God's people are standing at the foot of Mount Sinai and God himself is at the top of the mountain in thunder and lightning. The people are trembling in fear. They are convinced they're going to die because God is so awesome.

Listen to what Moses says to the people:

> *Do not be afraid. God has come to test you, so that the*
> *fear of God will be with you to keep you from sinning.*
>
> *(Exodus 20 v 20)*

There is our impossible command again: *Do not be afraid.* There is a wrong sort of fear. The people are terrified because they know that they do not have the resources in themselves to face God. They are looking within and so they feel scared.

But look carefully at the way they are to avoid fear. It is *the fear of God* that will keep them from sinning. The way to not be afraid is to fear God.

The solution to wrong fear is not no fear but right fear.

The fear of God is so powerful that it can drive out all other fears. This is the key—which raises the obvious question, what does it mean to fear God?

Fear God

This is a huge concept in the Bible. We don't have time to unpack it completely—but for now let's talk about it in terms of how big our view of God is.

Standard fear works like this: *I am small; the enemy is really big. Therefore I am scared. Aarrgghh.*

Godly fear looks like this: *I am small; the enemy is really big. But God is bigger; therefore I fear him.*

That is the key shift in our understanding. We stop looking at how small we are, we stop looking at how big the enemy is—and we start looking at the sheer greatness of God. This is what God means when he says, "Don't be afraid".

Our natural tendency is to shrink God and rely on ourselves. That is what leads to a life of fear and anxiety. It is the foolishness of human sin. We place ourselves on the throne and then wonder why we are so stressed all the time. We are trying to sit in a place where we were not designed to sit. We are not heavy enough to cope with the reality of life and death.

But to fear God means to recognise how heavy and awesome *he* is and to let him take his rightful place. Replacing our fears with the fear of God means we look beyond ourselves, beyond our situations, to the One who has all power.

God does not puff us up and tell us we have the power inside us. He does not belittle our problems and tell us to stop making a fuss. No, he lifts up our eyes so that we might see *him*. He calls us to be humbled, awed, thrilled and delighted by his great power. To fear God doesn't mean to be afraid of him but to see him as he really is, in all his awesome majesty and power. It means to revere him and to obey him.

> *Let all the earth fear the LORD;*
> *let all the people of the world revere him.*
>
> *(Psalm 33 v 8)*

Here is the God who created and loves the world. Rather than punishing us for our defiant acts of self-reliance, he gave his Son, Jesus, to save us. Jesus has faced our sin, he has faced our death, and he has faced our enemies with all the resources of God. He died and rose again to win victory for us.

When you turn from trusting yourself and instead rely on God's power, you become his child. You do not fear him as an enemy but know him as an awesome Father.

Here is where the battle lies—replacing your fears with this far greater fear. Standard fear leaves us uncertain and anxious. Godly fear leaves us confident and at peace.

God's good intention
Let me push this one stage further. Did you notice in 2 Corinthians how the apostle Paul talked about our "beyond our ability" experiences:

> *We were under great pressure, far beyond our ability*
> *to endure, so that we despaired of life itself ... But this*
> *happened that we might not rely on ourselves but on*
> *God, who raises the dead.*
>
> *(2 Corinthians 1 v 8-9)*

He said that those things *happened* so *that* they might not rely upon themselves but on God. Do you hear the intentionality in what Paul says? There was a reason why Paul experienced those situations, and it was to drive him to rely on God.

"Imagine you lived the whole of your life without ever facing anything that was beyond your ability. You would never learn to rely on God and would live with the delusion that you didn't need him. God loves you far too much to allow you to live like that."

———

IMPOSSIBLE
COMMANDS

The terrifying situations we face are an opportunity for us to learn this same lesson: that we might learn to rely on God and not on ourselves.

Imagine you lived the whole of your life without ever facing anything that was beyond your ability. You would never learn to rely on God and would live with the delusion that you didn't need him. God loves you far too much to allow you to live like that. And so God, as a loving heavenly Father, brings you to situations that are beyond your ability so that you will rely on him.

When we feel our weakness, when we feel afraid—it is a God-given opportunity to discover in a fresh way the power and love of God.

I'm not saying it's easy. Many of us know the reality of sleepless nights and painful tears. We know the questions that spin around our minds and the fears that haunt our dreams.

But our inability is an opportunity to learn to fear God. He is heavy enough. He has the resources.

A case study

There were three friends—Shadrach, Meshach and Abednego—living in a foreign land called Babylon. They were God's people, but God seemed to be fairly distant, and a man called King Nebuchadnezzar seemed to be in charge. The king gave an order one day that everyone in his kingdom must bow down and worship the statue he had made. Anyone who refused would be thrown into a blazing furnace.

Shadrach, Meshach and Abednego faced a choice. Would they bow down to the statue or would they remain true to God?

I imagine they had sleepless nights. I imagine that they were very, very afraid. King Nebuchadnezzar was a very big enemy with a lot of power, and they were very small. The situation was far beyond their ability to cope with, and you could hardly have blamed them if they caved in under the pressure. But they reasoned differently. They modelled what it means to fear God. They refused to bow down, and when King Nebuchadnezzar confronted them, this is what they said:

King Nebuchadnezzar, we do not need to defend ourselves before you in this matter. If we are thrown into the blazing furnace, the God we serve is able to deliver us from it, and he will deliver us from Your Majesty's hand. But even if he does not, we want you to know, Your Majesty, that we will not serve your gods or worship the image of gold you have set up.

(Daniel 3 v 16-18)

Did you hear that? They are not looking at Nebuchadnezzar. He is a very strong enemy, but they are looking beyond him. They are looking to God, and they are confident that he is able to save them.

This is not self-confident heroism—I imagine that they were terrified. Rather, they were choosing to not give in to fear but instead to fear God. They were afraid, but they didn't allow that fear to stop them from obeying God. He is able. That is what they needed to know.

The Four Steps
I can't

I don't think this will be a hard step for most of us when it comes to this command. We so often find ourselves afraid. Many of us get very anxious and have all sorts of reasons for it. The situations we face are sometimes so hard and big that there seems to be no possible way through. Other fears may seem smaller but still leave us with a knot in our stomach or tossing and turning at night.

I want to encourage you to be honest with God about that. Tell him exactly how you feel. Tell him your fears and what they do to you. He is not asking you to be brave. He is not asking you to "man up". What a ridiculous and thoroughly unhelpful concept that is. We get scared because we are small.

I'm sorry

This step is harder. We often want to excuse ourselves from blame in this area of anxiety. I know that there are all sorts of causes of our anxiety, and it is an extremely complex area. Some of us will need to seek help to enable ourselves to process things and make progress in this area. If that's you, why not plan to talk to someone about it soon—maybe your pastor, a doctor or a mature Christian friend?

But I want to gently say that we will not make progress if we fail to own our part in our anxieties. We are not simply victims, but we all choose day by day to try and place ourselves on the throne of our lives. We were not designed for that position, and we do not have the resources to cope with that position. We need to confess the ways in which we have looked to ourselves rather than to God.

We don't confess in order to condemn ourselves. We confess because Jesus was condemned in our place and in him we find forgiveness for our sin.

Please help

Then we need to ask for help. *Please help me not to be afraid anymore. Please help me to see you as you really are. Please help me to see reality more clearly. Please let me see that you are bigger—far bigger—than anything or anyone I'm afraid of.*

If God commands us not to be afraid, he will also provide us with all the resources we need to keep that command.

If you are trusting in Jesus, then God is not against you. His commands are not against you. He is on your side and in your corner, promising you power to do battle with anxiety and fear.

The Holy Spirit is God's wonderful gift to his struggling children. He loves it when we ask.

Let's go
The fight is on. This is not a quick fix, but I hope you can begin to see at least where the battle lies. We're not being told to try and be brave. We're not being told to stop making a fuss. That is not the battle. No, the battle lies in seeing God more clearly. That is where we need to focus our efforts. The battle lies in replacing our fears with a greater fear. It is a battle that rages every single day as the size of the enemies we face sometimes seems to be so enormous. We feel the seesaw tipping, and we find ourselves out of control.

Right there, in that moment, is where the battle rages and where you need to fight.

The anxious thought is not a sin. It is a crossroad that presents you with a choice. It is an opportunity. The key issue is, what will you do with that anxious thought?

Will you let those worries drive you away from God and into the jaws of despair? Or will you let those worries drive you into the loving arms of your powerful Father?

Lift your eyes beyond the anxiety and see the greatness of God. Get a trusted Christian friend to stand with you in the battle. It is hard to let others know of our struggles but we need them in this fight.

For many of us this is a battle that rages with ferocious intensity. I'm not saying this is easy. But with honesty, confession and the power of the Holy Spirit, we can make progress.

"Do not be afraid ... for I am with you."
           (Genesis 26 v 24; Isaiah 43 v 5; Jeremiah 1 v 8)

8. Love one another

Jesus said ... "A new command I give you: love one another. As I have loved you, so you must love one another."

(John 13 v 34)

In one sense, love is very easy. Anyone can do it. In fact, everyone does do it. You don't have to be commanded— it just happens naturally. Someone (or something) lovely comes across your path, and you find yourself reacting with love.

For example, at a very superficial level I love ice cream (actually, my love of ice cream runs pretty deep, but the point still remains). I have never been commanded to love it. I have never needed that command. I just love it.

On the other hand, I'm not keen on sweetcorn. I tolerate it (now that I'm a grown-up), but if you commanded me to love it, I would think you very strange. It's simply not lovely to me.

This is what we are going to call "reactive love". I react with love towards ice cream, but I just tolerate sweetcorn.

If that was what Jesus had in mind, there would be no need for this command, but it won't surprise you to discover that he's talking about something very different: not a love that reacts to what is lovely but a love that moves towards the unlovely. This is *active* love, not reactive.

That sort of love is far beyond our natural ability. Active love is Christ-like love—loving the unlovely as Jesus did—and that's impossible!

Damp feet

We will need to be careful not to simply think of love in an abstract way. After all, most people like the idea of love in a general sense and think that more of it would make the world a better place.

But Jesus has no interest in an abstract view of love. He has something far more concrete in mind, so this is where we need to start.

Bear in mind that the first men who heard this command still had damp feet. Jesus had just shown them in the most concrete way possible what love really looks like. When Jesus washed his disciples' feet, he put love on display with far more than just words. He took the initiative; he moved towards them; he took the risk and he stooped down to do good. Here is active love. Jesus is not reacting to something he sees in them; he is acting out of his love for them.

The logic of love

The logic of this command is inescapable. Notice the word "so" as you read it again...

*A new command I give you: love one another. As I have loved you, **so** you must love one another.*

(John 13 v 34)

Do you see the logic? Jesus has loved us in a particular way, and *so* we must love one another in the same way.

The command to love one another is set in the context of the love that Jesus has for us. You cannot separate the two. In fact, the love of Jesus provides both the *reason* for us to love one another and the *example* of what it means to love one another. If we don't feel the compelling power of this logic, we will not love one another in the way Jesus intends.

Only this will enable us to move beyond reactive love and begin to pursue lives of active love—that is, love that acts.

Let's take a closer look at the story to see exactly what happened. It starts with the evening meal and a fascinating comment about Jesus in verse 3. Look at what he knows. Here is where his love starts:

*Jesus knew that the Father had put all things under
his power, and that he had come from God and was
returning to God...*   *(John 13 v 3)*

Loved freely

This is key. Jesus' love flows from a place of absolute
confidence about his identity. He knows who he is. He
knows that he has been given all power and that his
Father loves him. He has nothing to prove. Jesus isn't
desperately hoping that people will like him. He doesn't
wash their feet in order to enhance his own reputation, or
to strengthen his own position, or to win their approval.
He doesn't love them because of what's in it for him. He
freely chooses to love them because he is free to choose.

Jesus didn't have to wash their feet. He didn't need to
wash their feet. He had all power and was utterly secure.
That means his action was purely driven by love. From
that place of power, Jesus freely chose to love. This is
active love.

All too often, I act in a loving way towards people because
I want to be accepted. I want to be affirmed and approved
of. My love can often come from a place of insecurity and
fear. I love in a way that boosts my self-esteem and my
sense of worth.

When we find ourselves in that place, we can quickly
become enslaved. We become paranoid about what
people think of us. We need people to compliment us
and tell us how great we are. We favour the people who

we think of as more important because their approval means more to us than the approval of others.

Jesus isn't like that. In contrast to how we often behave, his actions here are breathtakingly beautiful. When Jesus loves, he is completely free from any insecurity or need of approval. That means he doesn't favour the rich or the powerful, the influential or the popular. He is free to love anyone—even his unimpressive disciples with filthy feet.

As I have loved you, so you must love one another.

(John 13 v 34)

Here is where it starts for us. First we will need to be clear on who we are in Christ. We need to understand that God has done extraordinary things for us. We are his precious and beloved children. He has given us all things. We have nothing to prove. As we breathe in that reality, we are breathing in the oxygen that means we are free to start to really love people.

The more we know who we are, the freer we will become to love. Active love starts here.

Loved downwardly

From that place of complete security, look at what Jesus does. Notice the key word that links verse 3 to verse 4. Jesus knew he had all power...

*... **so** he got up from the meal, took off his outer clothing, and wrapped a towel round his waist. After*

*that, he poured water into a basin and began to wash
his disciples' feet, drying them with the towel that was
wrapped round him.*   *(John 13 v 4-5)*

Here is what Jesus does with all power. He does not use
it for his own advantage. He does not push his way to the
top. He willingly stoops down. *Down.*

That is the direction in which active love moves: it moves
downwards. Jesus isn't reaching up and grasping for
more and more power—he is moving down. Jesus isn't
moving towards what is attractive—he is moving down
to serve the needy.

This goes so radically against all we have ever been taught.
Every child knows of games where "up" is good and
"down" is bad. Everyone wants to be "king of the castle".
"Incy wincy spider" wanted to climb *up* the water spout.
In snakes and ladders, you want to climb up the ladders.
Everything is about moving up—and reactive love fits
perfectly into that view of the world. I will love things that
help me move up. I will love the people who make my life
better and easier and happier. Reactive love loves up.

But Jesus isn't like this. Christ-like love loves downwards.

Jesus doesn't love us because we are so attractive. The
picture of filthy feet is far more accurate. Jesus loves
those who are not lovely. Our sin is like filthy clothes
that we wear. His love does not start with something
attractive in us but with something powerful within
Jesus. This powerful love drives Jesus down to take the

very lowest place—even the place of a slave. Jesus loves downwardly and he calls us to do the same.

To love like this will cost. It won't happen naturally; it will need deliberate and costly action. It will be hard to love people that we don't find lovely.

Stop and think for a moment: who could you invite into your home for dinner? It's easy to love the people who can repay you for your kindness. But who could you love today who will never be able to repay you? Who could you choose to serve?

Loved riskily
Washing their feet is more than simply a nice thing that Jesus does for his disciples. He is taking a big risk.

In that moment of foot-washing, Jesus chose to move towards his disciples. He didn't wait for them to make the first move. (Let's face it, he would still be waiting now.) Instead, he took the initiative. He crossed the room and, as he did so, he broke down a barrier that needed to be broken.

Jesus went from a place of comfort to a place of vulnerability. That is what love does. It's definitely not the easy road, and it doesn't feel comfortable to us.

Imagine you were one of the disciples. It's tempting to sentimentalise the story and picture a warm, fuzzy moment as Jesus washes your feet—but I'm not so sure. I imagine it was extremely awkward. Surely the disciples felt uncomfortable and embarrassed about their filthy feet. After all, how would you react if someone approached you to wash *your* feet?

Peter certainly couldn't cope with it all. He was sitting and watching the events unfold, and when Jesus came to him he refused.

> *[Jesus] came to Simon Peter, who said to him, "Lord, are you going to wash my feet?"*
>
> *Jesus replied, "You do not realise now what I am doing, but later you will understand."*
>
> *"No," said Peter, "you shall never wash my feet."*
>
> *Jesus answered, "Unless I wash you, you have no part with me."*   *(John 13 v 6-8)*

It has to be this way. Love crosses the room, stoops down and serves. Peter needed to be served by Jesus. He needed to be washed by Jesus. Here is real love, and it creates relationships that are deeper than anything that normal human love can build.

This is how Jesus loves. He takes a risk. He moves forward.

Keep out

There are far too many walls within our churches. Every wall that we build is a symptom of what is wrong with humanity. From the famous walls of the world to the fence I put up round my garden, the message is the

"Active love is Christ-like love—loving the unlovely as Jesus did—and that's impossible!"

———————

IMPOSSIBLE
COMMANDS

same: *keep out*. I like my neighbours, and I'm happy to be friendly to them; but I don't want them in my space. Everything is fine as long as we stay at a distance; I would rather you weren't in my garden.

We can do this in church all the time. There are walls between the young and the old, between the rich and poor, between the in-crowd and the out-crowd. And we can be far too tolerant of these walls.

Love gets up, crosses the room and takes a risk. It often feels uncomfortable—that's a sign you're probably doing something right—and it begins to build something extraordinary. Picture this imaginary story...

Jake was 15 years old. He was happy in the youth group but found church pretty hard going. One day he made a bold and radical move—he turned up at the Monday night prayer meeting. It was unknown territory for teenagers, but Jake decided to give it a go. It was exactly what he expected: mostly older people and not really his cup of tea, but Jake kept going. He tried to join in and sometimes prayed out loud. It seemed a bit of a waste of a Monday evening, but little did he know the impact he was having on 81-year-old Ron.

Every time Jake prayed, Ron had a tear in his eye. A friendship began to grow. It was a friendship built across the barricade. It was a wall-smashing friendship. It was a risky move, but Jake began to find his heart moved with genuine love for Ron. He began to do a weekly shopping trip for Ron and, when Ron became ill, Jake would read to him from the Bible. At Ron's funeral, Jake really cried. He didn't regret one single moment he had spent with Ron.

Loved completely

Let's go back to the foot-washing story to notice one final thing.

> *[Jesus] poured water into a basin and began to wash his disciples' feet, drying them with the towel that was wrapped round him.* (John 13 v 5)

There is a completeness to the action of Jesus here. He doesn't just pour the water. He doesn't leave his disciples dripping wet. He does it all as he dries their feet with the towel.

This is a maximal love—not seeking to do the bare minimum that might be considered "loving" but looking for the fullest and most complete way possible to express love.

Of course, in just a few chapters time in John's Gospel, Jesus would go the cross. The washing of the disciples' feet suddenly took on a whole new significance as Jesus died to wash us clean of all our filth. He did it all. He didn't get it started and leave us to finish it. His final cry as he dies on the cross was:

> *It is finished.* (John 19 v 30)

That is love. Complete. Full. Vast. Magnificent.

That is how Jesus loves us. Can you imagine if *we* loved like that?

We can practice this in the small, everyday things of life. Lesley used to be our church administrator. She was great at this. I would come into the office and ask if there were any stamps. Her response wasn't, "Yes, in the third drawer down". Instead, she would take the letter, put a stamp on it and then take it to the post box. There was a completeness in her desire to serve others.

I love the idea of thinking about the maximum love I could show to a person. Yes, I know it can become overwhelming, but it can also be exciting.

The Four Steps
I can't
Here's a whole list of questions about the people in your church. Please take the time to think through them. As with 15-year-old Jake and 81-year-old Ron, this could be life-changing.

Who are the people in church you don't find attractive and who feel more of a drain than a joy? Who are the people you try to avoid? Who are the people that make your life harder? Or perhaps the people you just don't engage with because they are so different to you?

Why do you struggle to engage with them? Is it fear of people who are different? Is it laziness? It's always easier to speak to the people we like.

Do you struggle with insecurity and find yourself craving the approval of others?

Are there resentments that you hold towards others? Are there past hurts that you struggle to get past?

Be honest with God. Try and be as specific as you can about how hard you find this command.

I'm sorry

Now take time to confess the attitudes you have uncovered. You may well have found deeply-held resentments or prejudices that lurk in your heart. Confess those to God.

You may have discovered insecurities which mean you are finding it hard to believe that you are secure in God's love. Confess that to the Lord. Do you find it hard to believe that Jesus loves you? Perhaps, like Peter, it makes you feel uncomfortable.

It is essential that we breathe deeply the truth that Jesus loves us. He loves you *freely*. He doesn't have to, but he chose to. He loves you *downwardly*. He stooped to a cross to clean you of all of your filth. He has taken the *risk* of coming to love you where you are. And he loves you *completely*, doing all that is necessary to make you completely clean. That is his active love for you.

As you confess your sin, know that Jesus washes you clean. Before we can be set free to actively love people, we must understand our identity in Jesus. You are secure and loved because of Jesus. You have nothing to prove. God is your heavenly Father, who approves of you. Love starts here.

Please help
Now take the issues you have identified and begin to pray. When God commands you to love others, it's because he is going to give you the power to do it. You don't have to look within yourself; you have to look to the One who gave the command in the first place.

Ask God specifically to help you to love the people you find it hard to love. Part of the Holy Spirit's work is to produce *love* (Galatians 5 v 22). So ask him. I'm not talking about praying generally that we would be more loving. I'm talking about praying about specific people that you want to learn to love.

Think about the love that Jesus has shown you. Who can you love freely? How could you love downwardly? Riskily? Completely? Ask for joy in obedience. Ask for God to do remarkable things.

Let's go
Now make a plan for what you're going to do. Remember that love is active: it *does* things. So don't sit around waiting to be hit with a wave of fuzzy, loving feelings. You might be waiting a long time. Rather, begin to actively love people. There are a hundred and one things you could try. Get creative and generous in your love for others.

Check out these contrasts and see if they spark any specific ideas in your mind.

Reactive love chooses to spend time with the people who have something to offer. They make me feel good, or they make me laugh, or we enjoy spending time together. But active love is not driven by feelings; it is looking for those in need—perhaps those who don't have much to offer. Active love doesn't act in a patronising and smug way (in order to make myself feel better) but out of a genuine desire to help with the needs of others.

Who do you love in your church family? Who could you decide to start to love? How are you going to actively show that love to them?

Reactive love will cool off pretty quickly if someone is not meeting my needs. It will get annoyed and move on to look elsewhere. But active love will persevere with people and will push through the struggles. When someone hurts me, active love will drive me back to them, not away from them.

Is there anyone with whom you have a cooled relationship? How could you move towards them in love? With a text? A coffee? An apology?

Reactive love will tend towards being a bit careless in relationships. It will make promises in the heat of the moment, but when that moment has passed, then the promises can be dropped. Active love is consistent and faithful. It does what it says it will do—just as Jesus loved his disciples completely.

Where could you make a commitment to love someone? Not in a one-off sense, but in an ongoing and persistent way? By praying for someone? By meeting with someone?

So what could you do? I hope that when you begin to think about it, you might see exciting opportunities to love as Jesus loved.

It will feel risky; you might be rejected; you might even wonder why you bothered. But keep in mind that the reason is that you want to obey Jesus and to love as he loved you.

> *A new command I give you: love one another. As I have loved you, so you must love one another.*
>
> *(John 13 v 34)*

9. Give cheerfully

It would be wrong to suggest that only people who follow Jesus will ever be generous. That would be ridiculous. But following Jesus does challenge us to a different sort of generosity—a joyful, sacrificial and glorious generosity, and that is way beyond our ability.

> *Each of you should give what you have decided in your heart to give, not reluctantly or under compulsion, for God loves a cheerful giver.* (2 Corinthians 9 v 7)

When I was little, I loved buying presents for my mum and dad. I shudder to think of the rubbish I bought them over the years: a hideous hand-carved candle that was never lit; a miniature copper kettle that collected dust for years and years; endless packets of potpourri. The list goes on (and on). I loved finding things and wrapping them up—and then watching their faces as they opened the present.

But here's what makes it all so strange. I had no money of my own. In order to buy them presents, I had to ask them to give me the money first. So I used *their* money to buy them something that they really didn't need (and in most cases didn't want). And here's the cool part: they were delighted to do it.

They enabled me to enjoy the pleasure of giving, even though it had all come from them in the first place.

That is the dynamic that operates when we give to God. There's a great example of this in the Old Testament. King David asks the people to give generously towards the work of building the temple (which will be done by David's son Solomon). David starts the generous train rolling with a huge gift out of his own personal treasure. He then calls on the people to follow his example and to give generously. There's a wonderful response as the leaders, and then the people, give willingly to the work. We might be tempted to stand in awe at this extravagant act of generosity—but that would miss what was really happening.

King David then prays, and his prayer expresses the dynamic that is really at work:

> *But who am I, and who are my people, that we should be able to give as generously as this? Everything comes from you, and we have given you only what comes from your hand.*   *(1 Chronicles 29 v 14)*

God doesn't need our money. He doesn't need anything from us. He isn't sitting in heaven hoping that his plans won't fail through lack of resources. That's not how generosity works in the Bible. Rather, God delights to involve us in his purposes. He gives to us in order that we can then give to him. Our giving should not be a cause of smug pride. When we act like that, it shows we think that we've done God a favour. Rather, our giving should lead us to the sort of "who am I?" humility that King David expressed in his prayer.

Privilege

When we see things that way, we will start to understand how the apostle Paul can talk about a group of Christians who...

> ... *urgently pleaded with us for the privilege of sharing in this service to the Lord's people.*
>
> *(2 Corinthians 8 v 4)*

These were people experiencing severe trials and extreme poverty (2 Corinthians 8 v 2), but they didn't assume that that excused them from getting involved in giving. They were overflowing with joy in Jesus, and that led to great generosity—not just with their money but with the whole of their lives. That was something that God had done in them. And it's something he can do in us too.

We're back again at our main theme of joyful obedience. The people in David's day gave willingly. The church in Paul's day was pleading for the privilege of giving.

That's the sort of obedience that only God can produce in us. That's when obedience becomes a joy.

But let's be honest—it often doesn't feel that way.

Think about being asked to support the work at church, or receiving an email with news of desperate need in another part of the world. How do our hearts react? Do our hearts beat with excitement at the privilege of being able to give? Probably not. More likely we feel a sense of guilt. We know that we *should* give, but we have lost sight of the magnificent truth that we *can* give.

One of the dangers as we try to obey God's commands is that we settle for guilt-driven obedience—and guilt is a pretty powerful motivation to do things. There are many things in life that we do because we feel guilty about them. Guilt can make people give significant amounts of money if you pull at the right heartstrings and turn up the emotional heat.

But that is not a gospel motivation, and it's not what God saved us for. If we belong to Jesus, then it would be tragic for us to settle for guilt-driven giving. God has something far better for us in this area of generosity: something joyful, something exciting, and, yes, something impossible.

The grab reflex

Babies are born with a grab reflex. Hold out your little finger, and a tiny baby will grasp hold of it. In a newborn this is very cute, but as the child grows, the grabbing instinct becomes a little more troubling. Once they begin to pick up some language, the word "MINE" quickly accompanies the actions, and then the problems really start...

We can see it in children, but the reality is that those instincts still lurk deep within our own hearts. We learn more subtle ways to do it, but the basic desire remains. We still want to grab things for ourselves.

This is greed. It is the insatiable appetite for more. Whether that is money or recognition or power or pleasure or possessions—we want more. Why do we behave this way?

Many of us instinctively believe that there's a "happy place" somewhere out there, and we're constantly told that the key that opens the door of Happy Land is the key called "more". It's weird because often we aren't even sure what we're seeking more of. We just believe that more is the key to our happiness, so we keep reaching and grabbing.

Obviously, if "more" is the key to happiness, then I will find it very hard to be generous. It doesn't take a genius to work out that when I give things away, I end up with less, not more.

Generosity works against the natural instinct that all of us have to grab more.

Jesus warned pretty bluntly about this tendency in us.

> *Watch out! Be on your guard against all kinds of greed;*
> *life does not consist in an abundance of possessions.*
>
> *(Luke 12 v 15)*

Jesus says we've got it all wrong. To experience life as it's meant to be lived, we need a completely new perspective. *More* is not the key: *generosity* is.

Jesus follows up his warning with a story to make the point...

More than enough

The ground of a certain rich man yielded an abundant harvest. He thought to himself, "What shall I do? I have no place to store my crops."   *(Luke 12 v 16-17)*

This man has a problem. He has too much grain but has nowhere to store it all. Don't you just hate it when that happens? "Now what am I supposed to do?"

Of course, it all depends what you see when you look at the great heap of grain sitting in front of you. If that grain represents life to you, then the answer is obvious. If that grain speaks to you of early retirement and a life of comfort and pleasure, then there's only one thing to do.

This is what I'll do. I will tear down my barns and build bigger ones, and there I will store my surplus grain. And I'll say to myself, "You have plenty of grain laid up for many years. Take life easy; eat, drink and be merry."
(Luke 12 v 18-19)

It's so obvious. It seems so wise. This man is doing what so many in our world are desperately pursuing. He has more than enough. That's the dream, right? That's

Happy Land, right there. But the man is a fool. He has tied his life to his grain—and here is God's verdict:

You fool! This very night your life will be demanded from you. Then who will get what you have prepared for yourself? (Luke 12 v 20)

The man has ignored God. In fact, as the man makes his plans, God doesn't even get a look in—and that's not wise. In fact, it's the heart of folly. You think that happiness is found in more, but the reality is that only death lies there.

[Jesus says,] "This is how it will be with whoever stores up things for themselves but is not rich towards God." (Luke 12 v 21)

Being "rich towards God" is what matters, not being rich in material wealth. Happiness is not found in more possessions but in more of God.

The real problem with greed is that as we grab for more in this world, it's impossible for us to also grab hold of God. It's one or the other.

We need a power greater than ourselves to help us see that happiness is found not in stuff but in God. We need someone who is strong enough to save us from our love of possessions and replace it with a deep love for God.

His name is Jesus. He never pursued more: not possessions or comfort or fame or power. Jesus never grabbed but instead let it all go. And he did it because his relationship with his Father was more than enough for him.

Only Jesus can save us. Only he can change our hearts. Only he can help us see that God is more than enough to satisfy us.

When Jesus begins to change our hearts, something remarkable happens. Just imagine how different that story might have been. Let's have a go at re-telling it. Let's imagine that the man has had his heart changed...

A better way

The ground of a certain rich man yielded an abundant harvest. He thought to himself, "What shall I do? I have no place to store my crops." (Luke 12 v 16-17)

So he prayed. "Father, thank you for this extraordinary crop that you have entrusted to me. Please help me to use it wisely." Then he invited the poor and the hungry, the crippled and the lame to come and eat. They feasted together and experienced the love of God in an extraordinary way. It was wonderful! So the next year the man planted more. He worked hard. His back ached and his hands blistered but it was worth it, because every year he had even more to give.

Then one night the man died. It was the night that God came to take him home. "Well done, my faithful servant. Come and share in what has been prepared for you."

"God doesn't need our money.
He doesn't need anything from
us. God delights to involve us
in his purposes. He gives to us
in order that we can then give
to him."

———————

IMPOSSIBLE
COMMANDS

In the original story, the huge pile of grain represented all of the man's hopes and dreams. He looked at the grain and saw happiness and comfort. His life was tied up there, so obviously he could not give it away. The tragedy was that his abundant wealth could do nothing to save him from death or make him right with God.

But in our reimagining of the story, the man has a whole new heart. The grain now represents an enormous opportunity to do good.

When God commands us to be generous, it's not because he wants us to be miserable. It's because he wants us to realise that we have more than enough in him.

The Four Steps
I can't
Sometimes we can try and pretend to be generous but actually use that to cover up what is really going on. It's easy to be generous with stuff that we aren't bothered about.

If I have a box of *Liquorice Allsorts*, I'm more than happy to share it. If you walked into the room, you might well be convinced that I am a generous sort of guy. But the reality is that I'm not a big fan of liquorice. The bigger question comes when I have a box of *Maltesers*. That's when generosity gets real.

God isn't asking us to be generous with what we have to spare. God isn't asking us for token acts of generosity that salve our conscience and make us feel better. He is asking for generosity that really costs us: generosity that leaves us with significantly less than we had before.

For some of us, this means being generous with our money, but there are other ways to be generous too. Generous with our time. Generous with our comfort. Generous with our resources.

Where do you find it hardest to be generous? What stops you being generous? Is it a fear that your happiness might be threatened?

Think right now about a radical and costly act of generosity: something that is far beyond your comfort zone. What is it that makes you fearful of doing that?

I'm sorry

We all love to label things as "MINE". As a child I was given a set of stickers that said, *This belongs to Jonty*. I stuck them on everything (including my brother's stuff, which didn't go down so well). That is our instinct. It is *my* house, *my* car, *my* money, *my* clothes, and so it goes on. But it's profoundly wrong.

The reality is what King David showed us right back at the start of this chapter. Ultimately, these things are not mine but God's—they all come from him. God gives to us so that we can then be generous.

We need to take time to say sorry to God for all the times when we store things up and call them "MINE".

Confess the ways in which your heart makes generosity impossible.

But don't beat yourself up. Instead, lift your eyes to Jesus.

Think of his amazing life. Think of all the ways that he gave. He gave his time, his energy, his power. Can you think of one miracle that Jesus did for himself rather than for others? No. Not one.

If I had all that power, I would at least use some of it for myself—but not Jesus. He is the perfectly generous man. Ultimately, Jesus gave his life for us. As you see the selfishness of your own heart, find hope in the death of Jesus for you. He died for all the times we have grabbed and not given. He died because we find riches in possessions rather than God. He died the death that we deserve, so that we can live a new life of generous love.

Please help

Remember, when God commands us to give generously, that command comes with all the power of God to bring about that change. He's not waiting with a big stick to force you into obedience. He's waiting with his powerful Holy Spirit to enable your obedience.

Allow this command to cause hope to rise within you. Think of the beauty of a generous life. Imagine the good that you could do with all the resources that God has given you.

Ask God to cause you to desire him more than anything, so that you can start to give more and more.

Until we find ourselves able to say that giving is a privilege, we will always find our generosity stunted and difficult. So, keep asking that God's wonderful Holy Spirit will change your heart.

The Holy Spirit is part of God's great generosity to us. Just hear the generosity oozing out of these words of Jesus:

> *If you then, though you are evil, know how to give good gifts to your children, how much more will your Father in heaven give the Holy Spirit to those who ask him!*
>
> *(Luke 11 v 13)*

God is so willing and ready to give us the help of his Holy Spirit, if only we will ask.

Let's go

Now is the time to take action. By this point, I hope we might even be excited at the thought of being generous. Think about your regular giving. Are you giving to your local church? Have you reviewed that recently?

Are there specific people that you could support? And as you give financially, you may well find that your interest, love and prayers grow too.

Perhaps you don't have a lot of disposable income. How can you be generous with your time? Or your possessions? Or your gifts?

The danger is that the needs can seem overwhelming, and our resources can feel so limited, but don't let that stop you making a start. If you're not sure how and where to give, why not fix up a time to have a chat with your church pastor about it?

God is not asking us to be reckless and unwise. Providing for ourselves and for our families is important. But my guess is that for most of us that's not the danger. I know for myself I'm far more likely to hold back rather than give generously.

The key to life is not the pursuit of more possessions. It is to start pursuing more of our wonderful God.

> *Each of you should give what you have decided in your heart to give, not reluctantly or under compulsion, for God loves a cheerful giver.* (2 Corinthians 9 v 7)

10. Be completely humble

In the UK people stand in a queue; in the US they wait in line; but wherever we are, it can be extremely stressful. Which is weird because we spend a decent chunk of our lives standing in queues. (I read once that we spend about six months over our lifetime queuing.) But although it's a common experience, we don't find it easy. There is a constant fear that someone might get ahead of us.

It happens in traffic jams. I look at the cars around me and make it my aim to stay in front of them. It happens in theme parks when you wait for hours and then someone tries to jump the queue (or even worse, someone comes along who has paid for the right to jump in at the front... aarrggh). But most of all it happens in superstores. There are few things in life more frustrating than choosing your checkout line poorly.

The desire to be first leads to a deeply stressful existence—but there is a very simple solution. It is so simple that you can even test this for yourself with a basic experiment. Next time you're in the superstore and it's really busy and you feel your stress levels rising, try this: turn to the person behind you and say, "Would you like to go in front of me?"

Suddenly you won't care any more about the speed of the various lanes. Yes, you'll be in the store for longer. Yes, others will have beaten you in the great checkout race. But the difference is that you won't care. You have chosen to put yourself last.

Because here is the beautiful secret of humility. Real freedom is found at the back of the line, not at the front.

In Ephesians 4, God commands us to...

> *be completely humble and gentle.*
>
> *(Ephesians 4 v 2)*

When God issued that command, he was calling us to a life at the back of the line—and that's a life of joyful and wonderful freedom. Although it sounds simple, obeying this command is actually impossible: but as we honestly admit our weakness, confess the wrong in our hearts and cry out to God for help, he will give us the power to start to obey him.

Queue-jumpers

Queue-jumping is nothing new; it has always been a part of human nature. When Jesus spotted it in his disciples, he called it out. There was an occasion when Jesus had just been teaching his disciples that they were going to

Jerusalem, where he would be mocked, spat on, flogged and killed. He had told them clearly that he would die and then rise again.

At the very moment that Jesus finished what he was saying, James and John (two of his disciples) came forward with a request. You can read it for yourself in Mark's Gospel:

> *"Teacher," they said, "we want you to do for us whatever we ask."* (Mark 10 v 35)

That seems to me to be a pretty bad way to start, but Jesus is patient and kind. So he asks them:

> *What do you want me to do for you?* (v 36)

That's the question of a servant. We will come back to that in a moment as it takes us to the heart of what true humility really looks like. But for now, let's look at what it is that James and John want.

> *Let one of us sit at your right and the other at your left in your glory.* (v 37)

The request is very clear. They have understood that Jesus is the King of God's kingdom, and they want to make sure they get in early with their bid for the best places. They are trying to push themselves to the front of the line.

We can all see that this is a nasty and ugly request, and yet, when I hear them, I know I see the same sort of attitudes lurking in my own heart. We want to be first.

Entitlement

The problem starts with a wrong view of self. Queue-jumping has at its root the basic assumption that I'm different to everyone else and therefore entitled to go to the front. Although I'm sure that James and John would never have put it this way, they are essentially saying that they're more important, more special, and more valuable than the other disciples. They have the right to be treated differently.

But they are completely wrong.

> *"You don't know what you are asking," Jesus said.*
> *"Can you drink the cup I drink or be baptised with the*
> *baptism I am baptised with?"* (v 38)

Jesus has a cup to drink that will be deeply painful. It is the cup of suffering that he will drink at the cross as he faces the wrath of God against sin. He has a baptism to undergo. It is the baptism of suffering that he will experience at the cross as he is submerged under the terrifying judgment of God.

Jesus has been explaining to James and John that he must die and then rise again. But they weren't really paying attention. Jesus asks them if they are able to drink this cup and they respond with a confident: "We can" (v 39).

Yep, we think we can probably handle that Jesus, no worries. They haven't got a clue what they're talking about. They don't think to ask for clarification on what Jesus means before they jump right in. No doubt they are picturing a victory cup and a baptism into glory. But they will learn, and they will suffer, but first they need to stop trying to jump the queue.

Go to the back

The other disciples are pretty annoyed with James and John (I think because they're worried that their own positions in glory might be damaged). So Jesus gathers them all together and teaches them the great principle of humility.

> *You know that those who are regarded as rulers of the Gentiles lord it over them, and their high officials exercise authority over them. Not so with you. Instead, whoever wants to become great among you must be your servant, and whoever wants to be first must be slave of all. For even the Son of Man did not come to be served, but to serve, and to give his life as a ransom for many.*
> (Mark 10 v 42-45)

Greatness in God's kingdom is found at the back of the line, not the front. It is found in the deliberate, willing, joyful choice to be a servant of all. The command to be humble is an exciting and inspiring way to view life.

The counter-revolution

This is completely counter to our natural way of thinking. Greatness in our world is measured by who comes first. No one remembers who came second.

There are plenty of competitions to find out who is the fastest, strongest, cleverest, richest and so on—but no one is interested in the "World's Weakest Man" competition. We're a culture that celebrates winners and ignores the losers. People do whatever it takes to get themselves to the front of the line. The need to be first is one of the factors that has led to an epidemic of stress in our culture.

The tragedy is that this same attitude has crept into churches. There are competitions to find the best preachers (seriously), worship leaders, churches and so on. Churches can begin to pursue success for the sake of looking impressive, and be jealous of other churches which, they fear, might be pushing ahead of them.

And if we're honest, we will find this creeping into our own hearts as well. We find small ways to push ourselves forward. We find it hard to be happy with the success of others because it makes us feel inferior and less valuable. Living like this is so stressful. For example, it's hard to be excited about the arrival of a new trombone player in the church band if I am the current trombone player and they turn out to be better than me. I will not serve them; I will compete with them—and I will find pleasure in their failure. It's horrible to see, but this is the opposite of humility.

The command to be humble is a challenge to my sense of entitlement. It is the willingness to let others go ahead; it is the letting go of my rights for the sake of someone else—and it is a choice.

"Next time you're waiting in line in the superstore, try this: turn to the person behind you and say, 'Would you like to go in front of me?'"

———————

IMPOSSIBLE
COMMANDS

Life in God's kingdom works completely differently. The action really is all at the back of the queue!

Life at the back

Right after the encounter with James and John comes another story. This is no accident. The sequence of stories is brilliantly crafted and put together to help us understand God's kingdom. We are immediately introduced to another man. His name is Bartimaeus, and he is blind. We meet him sitting by the side of the road begging. He is absolutely at the back of the line. He has nothing to offer, and he has no hope of ever pushing his way forward, but when he hears Jesus coming, he begins to call out:

Jesus, Son of David, have mercy on me!

(Mark 10 v 47)

The crowd want to shut him up. Why would Jesus be interested in a poor, blind beggar? *There are plenty of people ahead of you in the queue, Bartimaeus. You're not entitled to anything. Be quiet!*

But Bartimaeus keeps on shouting; and then something extraordinary happens.

The next two words are stunning. In Mark 10 v 49 we are told that *Jesus stopped*.

Jesus is on his way to complete the mission given to him by his Father. He is walking to Jerusalem, where he knows that he must die and rise again. It is the most important journey that any human being has ever taken.

What could possibly be important enough that Jesus would stop on his way to the cross?

Answer: blind Bartimaeus.

Here is the humility of Jesus summed up in two words: *Jesus stopped*. He's not thinking of himself. He doesn't make excuses: *Actually, I am very busy on my way to save the world*. He stops to serve a blind beggar.

Come to the front

We have seen that Jesus tells people at the front of the line to go to the back and learn to serve—but look at what he says to those at the back of the line; Bartimaeus gets a fast pass to the very front. Imagine him walking past all the crowds. They would have been open-mouthed at the sight of this man going ahead of them.

And then Jesus asks Bartimaeus a question. I wonder if this sounds familiar to you:

> *What do you want me to do for you?* (v 51)

It's the same question that Jesus asked James and John: the servant question. Jesus places himself, and all of the resources of heaven, at the disposal of this blind beggar. That's what humility looks like, right there.

Jesus doesn't presume to know what the man needs. He doesn't dish out a quick healing as he rushes past. No, he honours this blind man by asking him the question.

The blind man said, "Rabbi I want to see."

"Go," said Jesus, "your faith has healed you."
Immediately he received his sight and followed Jesus
along the road.   *(Mark 10 v 51-52)*

At the very moment that Jesus speaks, Bartimaeus is healed. His eyes are mended; he can see Jesus, and, right away, he starts to follow Jesus.

Jesus came to serve beggars. Jesus goes to those at the back of the line and says, *Come to the front so that I may serve you.*

Are you being served?
Is this your personal experience of Jesus? Do you realise that Jesus came to serve you? Even though we are only beggars who deserve to be at the back of the queue, Jesus calls us forward to serve us. Here it is in his own words (where he calls himself by the title "Son of Man"):

For even the Son of Man did not come to be served,
but to serve, and to give his life as a ransom for many.
(Mark 10 v 45)

He gave his life as a ransom for others. His death buys freedom for blind beggars. Jesus goes to the very back of the line to serve.

Why not pause for a moment to take that in? If you're a Christian, then Jesus the Servant went to the back of the line for you. He died for you. He bought freedom for you.

Let's thank him from the bottom of our hearts for dying for us. And if you're not quite sure whether you've ever put your trust in Jesus the Servant, why not talk to your pastor or another Christian about that? This would be a great time to start following Jesus.

Jesus has every right to demand that we serve him. But instead he first serves us. He asks us the servant question: "What do you want me to do for you?"

And then he calls us to do the same.

Completely humble

Obedience really matters. It really matters that we learn what it means to obey the command "Be completely humble and gentle" (Ephesians 4 v 2). This command is the secret to a whole heap of freedom and joy.

But it will require a real shift in the way we view ourselves. Rather than seeing ourselves as James and John saw themselves, we need to see ourselves as more like Bartimaeus. That is where humility starts, as we accept what the Bible says about who we truly are. It will mean giving up on the sense of entitlement. It will mean letting go of our rights.

That will then liberate us to joyfully and willingly push others ahead of us and then delight to see them going before us.

Even as I write this, it's clear that it's going to be quite a struggle—but it's worth the battle.

The Four Steps
I can't

Start by admitting how hard this is. The back of the queue is not an easy place to choose to go to. We have all sorts of fears about becoming a doormat. We worry that no one will appreciate us. We find it hard to give up status. We will probably miss out on things that could have been ours if we had just been a bit more pushy. We will find our rights shouting at us and telling how much we deserve to be appreciated and how much we are entitled to be at the front. We will discover that our culture is constantly telling us that we deserve to have everything. Perhaps the front of the line really does look very appealing to you.

It might help to consider where you find yourself jealous of others. Who is it, in particular, that you find yourself competing with? It can be so stressful to constantly be comparing ourselves to other people and trying to get ahead. Do you ever find yourself feeling just a little bit pleased when you hear of another Christian who has failed? I know that we would never say it out loud, but these thoughts can easily lurk within us.

If you have an up-front role within church, you will probably find this a battle. There will be a desire to impress people and "move forward" in your gifting. But our gifts are given to serve others, not to promote self.

I'm sorry

It takes humility to admit you're wrong, and it takes humility to say you're sorry. Take time to confess the sin you discovered in Step One.

Perhaps the contrast of James and John with blind Bartimaeus might help us. James and John could not see their desperate need and could only see what they thought they deserved. Bartimaeus, despite his blindness, saw the whole thing more clearly. He was not asking on the basis of his merit. He was asking for mercy.

He was asking Jesus to take pity on him in his terrible need—and Jesus stopped.

This is still true today. Anyone who knows their desperate need and calls out to Jesus for mercy will never be ignored. He stops to serve them.

The cry of Bartimaeus can become our cry: "Jesus, Son of David, have mercy on me!"

Before we can ever go to the back of the queue and serve others, we need to see how Jesus went to the back of the queue to serve us.

Confess your sin to him now and drink deeply of his mercy. When we feel how messed up we are, and how little we deserve, it is then that Jesus calls us to the front.

Please help

The power to be completely humble and gentle doesn't lie within us. The One who commands us to be humble is the One who enables us to live that out.

In the Bible book of James, chapter 3 v 13-18, we read about two types of wisdom. The first is earthly, and it is described as "bitter envy and selfish ambition" (v 14). That is the queue-jumping wisdom that wants to get to the front. But the second type of wisdom comes from heaven. It is "pure; then peace-loving, considerate, submissive, full of mercy and good fruit, impartial and sincere" (v 17). That is humility—the "humility that comes from wisdom" (v 13).

Notice that this wisdom comes from heaven, not from earth. If we are going to make any progress in this area, we need this heavenly wisdom. If humility comes from heaven, then we really need to ask for it. It is one of the good gifts that God loves to give. He empowers us by his Holy Spirit to live in humility.

Why not stop and ask him for humility right now? Talk to him about specific situations and people where you find it hard to be humble. Ask God to help you love to serve people.

Let's go

Humility is more than just an attitude; it's an action that needs to be lived out. So begin to take the action. Rather than competing with people, find ways to encourage others and push them ahead of you. Rather than looking down on people, make the first move to go and serve someone. You have nothing to prove. The King of the universe has served you.

Cultivate an attitude of humility. Perhaps when you are driving or shopping, be someone who lets others go ahead and, as you do, remind yourself that you are doing this because Christ served you.

In your workplace, where competition can often run wild, be the one who serves and lets others get the praise.

And no matter how far backwards you go, you will never find yourself going further back than Jesus.

> *Whoever wants to become great among you must be your servant, and whoever wants to be first must be slave of all. For even the Son of Man did not come to be served, but to serve, and to give his life as a ransom for many.*   *(Mark 10 v 43-45)*

11. Run away

Running away from danger is a basic human instinct. Which is precisely why six-year-old me was standing on a picnic table in the middle of a field.

What had started out as a simple game of football took a terrible turn when an enormous and savage dog ran onto the field. I still remember the panic as the dog fixed its eyes on me, bared its teeth and charged straight at me. I was terrified, but I knew I couldn't outrun it, so I leapt up onto a nearby picnic table. At which point the owner said those immortal words, "He's only being friendly". I was adamant that our definitions of "friendly" were not the same, and I breathed a sigh of relief as the crazed animal was dragged away.

When the danger presented itself, I didn't spend a long time considering the merits of the various options open to me. I just ran.

Flee sin

There are a number of places in the Bible where we are commanded to flee from sin. We are to flee sexual immorality (1 Corinthians 6 v 18) and idolatry (1 Corinthians 10 v 14) and the evil desires of youth (2 Timothy 2 v 22).

You find a similar idea in other places. Jesus talks about treating sin ruthlessly when he says that "if your hand causes you to stumble, cut it off" (Mark 9 v 43). The apostle Paul talks about "putting to death" sin (Romans 8 v 13 and Colossians 3 v 5).

These verses make it clear that sin is a dangerous and deadly enemy that must not be messed around with. This isn't hard to understand. Even six-year-olds know that you're supposed to run away from danger. In that sense, the command to flee from sin should be the most natural thing in the world.

But it isn't.

Despite the danger, rather than running, all too often we find ourselves attracted to sin. The very things we know are wrong are the things that we find utterly captivating. We don't see the danger.

Running away from something dangerous is easy and obvious: no problem there.

Running away from something harmless is harder to achieve, but it could be done.

But running away from something that is deeply attractive to us is impossible.

Here's the essence of our problem: sin isn't only dangerous; it's also highly attractive to us. That makes the command to flee sin an impossible command for us to obey.

I'm tired

My guess is that you find the constant battle with sin to be really tiring. I know I do. I keep making the same mistakes again and again. We find ourselves back in the same place over and over, and we feel utterly useless. Sometimes it makes us wonder if we're even Christians at all. We know what we're doing is wrong. We know we need to stop. We've tried and tried—but nothing happens.

This is what people sometimes call our "besetting sin". Or, to use the language of this book, we all have our particular "impossible sins". We've lost hope that we will ever see ourselves change in regard to these particular sins. We just can't do it.

We need to start by facing the reality of what we're up against. We must not underestimate sin.

If you're feeling hopeless, please don't give up. Remember that...

With man this is impossible, but not with God.

(Mark 10 v 27)

It's not going to be easy, but because Jesus died and rose again, in the end his power will win.

In this chapter we'll see that God can help us make a start.

Know the enemy

The first human baby ever born was a boy called Cain. You can imagine his parents looking at this beautiful baby and wondering what he would grow up to be. The reality of the story is not so beautiful, as this little baby boy grew up to be a murderer.

Cain became jealous of his younger brother, Abel. They had both offered sacrifices. Abel offered his gift with a heart of joyful dependence on God. This faith caused God to look on Abel with favour (faith always pleases God—consistently through the Bible). But Cain offered his gift with a wrong heart. Here is what God told him:

> *If you do what is right, will you not be accepted? But if you do not do what is right, sin is crouching at your door; it desires to have you, but you must rule over it.*
>
> *(Genesis 4 v 7)*

Crouching. Desiring. Like a snarling wild animal that wants to sink its teeth into you. Here is one of the first ways in which the Bible presents sin to us. It is personified as an ambushing enemy that has a whole range of desires and intentions to do us harm.

Sin is not simply the naughty things we do or the poor choices we make. We can easily trivialise sin and not see the reality of the enemy. Sin is a power that crouches nearby and looks for any opportunity to pounce. There is a "law of sin" that desires to exercise its rule in our lives (Romans 7 v 23). It seizes every opportunity it can find to take control of our lives.

Sin is a law that demands my obedience. It wages war against any good desires that I might have. It constantly offers me rewards if I will obey (pleasure, success, satisfaction, happiness) and threats if I don't (missing out, misery, failure).

This is the battle that the Bible says rages in us. There is no good intention that pops into our mind that is not immediately opposed by the power of sin at work in us.

I give money to a homeless man; then immediately I wonder whether anyone saw my good deed. I congratulate a work colleague for winning an award; then I undermine their success by joking about it. Even when I want to do good, my sinful heart stands ready to spoil it.

Defying gravity

Think about gravity. It is a power that continually operates on my body; it is a law that demands my obedience, and it frustrates my long-held ambition to fly. Any attempt I make to fly is immediately opposed by the power of gravity, which keeps pulling me down. Every time I jump, gravity steps in and says, "That's quite enough of that" as it wrenches me back to earth with a bump. It doesn't matter how hard I flap my arms; it just won't happen.

Of course, if I choose to abandon my desire to fly, then the battle stops and I just live as a prisoner of gravity. There's no more struggle.

So it is with sin. Every time I try to jump and obey God in some way, the law of sin springs into action to drag me back down. No matter how hard I try to flap my arms and make the effort, I cannot obey God unopposed. That's why it feels like a constant battle. It explains why choosing to obey God is just so hard. It also explains why choosing to sin feels so easy. When I make peace with sin and submit to its rule, then the war is over.

But the problem is that to make peace with sin is to allow death to rule. We were made to live according to God's law, not sin's law. God is a loving ruler who gives us life. Sin is a vicious master that pays us with death.

But despite all of that, sin still remains highly attractive.

Enticed
Fish find worms to be irresistibly attractive—why else would they swallow a vicious hook? Mice find cheese to be magnetically enticing—why else would they step on a deadly trap? And what worms are to fish and cheese is to mice, sin is to us.

The Bible uses precisely this sort of language to talk about what is happening when we sin. There's a powerful dynamic at work that we really must understand. For example, the book of James describes it like this.

Each person is tempted when they are dragged away by
their own evil desire and enticed. Then, after desire has
conceived, it gives birth to sin; and sin, when it is full-
grown, gives birth to death.   *(James 1 v 14-15)*

Sin has enormous pulling power. It tugs at us and drags
us in.

Imagine one day I try an experiment with one of my
children. I put my son in a room—and across the room
I put a table full of sweets. I then issue a command. It's
very clear and very simple. "You're not to eat the sweets."

I leave the room and close the door. What happens
next? Where is my child looking? His eyes are fixed on
the table: absolutely no question about it. In fact, if we
could watch a video, we would see his whole body leaning
towards the table. The sweets are actually pulling him.
He would shuffle his chair closer as the sweets reel him
in. He would soon be at the table and moving the sweets
around (I never said they couldn't be touched). It would
be a matter of moments before the wrappers came off
and the sweets were being shovelled in.

He is enticed. He is dragged. And soon he disobeys.

That is exactly what some sin feels like in my life. It reels
me in.

For my son to run away is impossible. The sweets are too
powerful. He might try and develop a strategy: he might
tie himself to his chair in a desperate attempt to obey.

What will his experience of obedience be? Joyful? No. It will be miserable. He is still staring at the table. Still longing for the sweets. Still desiring them.

The battle rages at the level of desire—not simply at the level of behaviour.

Here is where many Christians find themselves when it comes to the experience of obedience. They try as hard as they can to resist—and either give in or become miserable.

Sin is too attractive to us. Joyful obedience seems a million miles away.

A better way
There is a way I could make it easy for my boy to resist the sweets. He would just need something in the room that is more attractive. If Granny was on the other side of the room, suddenly the experience of resisting the sweets would completely change.

Granny "out-pulls" the sweets. She is more appealing. Now my boy can flee from the sweets and run to Granny, and do it joyfully.

That's the heart of how the Bible says we're supposed to obey God's command to flee sin. We need a gospel that can out-pull sin.

That is why, when the apostle Paul wrote, "Flee from sexual immorality" (1 Corinthians 6 v 18), he surrounded

"The problem is not simply
that we do wrong things; it
is that we *love* wrong things.
They pull on our hearts."

———————————

IMPOSSIBLE
COMMANDS

it with amazing truth about who we are in Christ. Check this out:

> *Do you not know that your bodies are members of*
> *Christ himself?* (1 Corinthians 6 v 15)

The good news is not just that Jesus saves our souls. It is not just that he forgives our sin. It is not that we will one day be disembodied spirits in heaven when we die. It is *much better* than that.

Your body, (yes, your actual physical body), is united with Christ.

Holy bodies

Sometimes, our culture can reduce our bodies to the level of desires that must be obeyed. Sin leaves us with a low view of the body; it leaves us frustrated and disappointed—but Jesus does the opposite. He places enormous value on our human bodies. Our bodies are united with him.

Here is more:

> *Do you not know that your bodies are temples of the*
> *Holy Spirit, who is in you, whom you have received from*
> *God?* (1 Corinthians 6 v 19)

This is massive. We have already seen this in chapter 6. The temple was awesomely holy.

But now we are told that our bodies are temples. God's Spirit lives in you. God is not embarrassed about your body, or squeamish, or disappointed. He sees our bodies as homes fit for himself.

Or what about this?

You are not your own; you were bought at a price.
Therefore honour God with your bodies.
(1 Corinthians 6 v 19-20)

You have been bought: a price has been paid. Jesus gave his body to buy yours. He has paid with his life.

In a world that is so confused about the body, and where so many find their bodies to be a source of deep pain and disappointment, here is a gospel with real pulling power.

Sin has brought death and weakness to your body. It makes great boasts, but it leaves us wasted. Jesus came to buy your body for himself: to unite himself to your body and to send his Spirit to live in you.

The Four Steps

Let's apply our four steps to the command to flee from sin. If you are tired in the battle, I hope this will help you to lift up your head and learn to fight in God's strength.

I can't

Remember we need to start with honesty—with being willing to admit that sin is too powerful for us to overcome on our own.

It would be awesome to be able to fly. Peter Pan was always a great inspiration to me as a child. But we need to get a little more honest about gravity.

We can make this same mistake all the time. We think that we can stop sinning if we just try hard enough— that if we flap our arms and put in enough effort, we can break free from the power of sin.

But we need to get a little more honest about sin. It is a powerful and attractive enemy that we do not have the power to defeat. When we flap our arms and we try to fly, it feels futile.

What are the sins that you find yourself returning to over and over again? What is it about those particular sins that have a hold on you? What are they offering?

How do you feel your powerlessness in this area? In what ways have you tried to beat sin on your own (e.g. tying yourself to that chair?!)?

Take the time to be honest with yourself about this before moving on to the next stage.

I'm sorry
We're not just victims here. We find that the problem is that we *love* sin. It's shocking that sin should be more attractive to us than Jesus. It shows how warped and distorted our hearts are that they would desire what God says is wrong.

The problem is not simply that we do wrong things; it is that we *love* wrong things. They pull on our hearts.

Learning to confess the wrong things we love, and not just the wrong things we do, is essential for us to grow in obedience. The problem is found at the level of our desires, and we need to allow the Holy Spirit to show us what we really love.

Sometimes, the reason we fail to make progress in battling sin is because we trivialise the problem and allow it to remain at the level of our behaviour. If I desire to commit adultery but don't act on it, then I might want to say that's not so bad. But Jesus says that the *desire* is the problem.

Learning to confess how much we love sin is painful, but here is where deep work is done.

Your body was bought at a price. Let me spell out the price for you so that you can really enjoy this truth again:

Jesus, the eternal Son of God, became a man. He had a real body. When he became a baby, he entered this world of sin. He felt the pull of sin and was tempted in every way (Hebrews 4 v 15). The law of sin tried to exert its rule over him. He experienced the battle but always loved his Father more than sin.

Every day, Jesus chose obedience to the law of God rather than obedience to the law of sin. That's a remarkable thing. He did that for us.

Then, at the cross, Jesus chose to offer himself in our place. He paid the price. For all the times we have loved and gone after sin, we deserve death—but Jesus paid that price in full. He experienced the full force of sin and of God's righteous anger at sin.

All of your sin and all of your love of sin have been paid for in full. Your sin is forgiven. This is a wonderful truth that every Christian can enjoy.

Please help
When God commands us to flee from sin, that command is accompanied by the power to bring about that change.

If we're going to escape the power of gravity, we need a rocket more powerful than gravity that will blast us out. If we're going to escape the power of sin, we need a rocket more powerful than sin that will blast us out. Jesus is that rocket.

When Jesus rose from the dead, his relationship to sin was completely changed. The battle was over. Romans 6 v 10 says that the "death he died, he died to sin once for all". In the resurrection, Jesus has smashed his way out of the power of sin for all eternity. He is not tempted by sin any more.

If we are trusting Jesus, then we are united with him and we can know that same power helping us in our battle.

We have not yet experienced the final resurrection and the complete defeat of sin. We still feel the pull, and we still experience the battle, but we can blast through that pull because Jesus has been raised.

Ask God, through his Spirit, to give you the power to flee from sin. Ask him to change your desires. There is a great old hymn—"Love Divine, all loves excelling"—that includes a line that captures this idea perfectly:

Take away my love of sinning.

What a prayer! That is how you ask for help.

Let's go

As we ask God for help, we then need to start to take some radical action. Fleeing is not a passive activity that just happens. We need to start to run away.

Is the problem your phone? Your computer? A flirty relationship at work? A place you go to? The after-work drinking culture? Jesus commands you to find ways to run from these things.

How often do we con ourselves into thinking that we can handle it, and it won't be a problem? The command is to run away—not to stay and hope it will be ok.

Think every day of that idea that sin is crouching at your door and looking to seize any opportunity that it can find to draw you back. Slam the door in sin's face. Cut off the opportunities for sin. The gospel is so good, and sin is such a liar. For the love of God, do something.

There is a lifelong battle ahead. Please don't think that it's going to be easy—but there is joy to be found in the battle for obedience. And on the days you fail, there is Jesus, who stands ready to forgive you, to pick you up and to help you go again.

Flee from sexual immorality.　　*(1 Corinthians 6 v 18)*

Flee from idolatry.　　*(1 Corinthians 10 v 14)*

Put to death ... whatever belongs to your earthly nature.　　*(Colossians 3 v 5)*

Conclusion:
Joyful obedience

I love walking along Striding Edge in the Lake District, England. It's a beautiful place, but it's also a little precarious. There is a narrow path, with a steep drop on either side. A little deviation to the left or right—and disaster awaits.

Walking the road of obedience can be a little like that. On one side is the steep slope of *joyless obedience*. This would often be called "legalism". This emphasises obedience in a way that makes it feel like a crushing burden. Legalism says it's our responsibility to obey God's commands, and we need to work hard. It leads to pride and self-righteousness when things are good, but shame and despair when we fail. There is little grace here.

But if you stumble the other way, you can easily tumble down the slope into *careless disobedience*. On this side of the mountain, we allow the message of God's grace to drive us to the conclusion that our obedience is not really that important. So it's nice if you can obey a little bit, but don't feel bad. Don't worry about sin because Jesus has forgiven you and loves you anyway.

Each of us will tend to fall into one of these errors. Some of us will even fall one way on one day, and then the other on the next. Many churches also have a tendency towards one of these mistakes. We need to be constantly alert to both dangers and instead seek to follow the path along the top of the mountain.

That's the path we've tried to explore in this book. It's the path of *joyful obedience*. It takes God's commands very seriously—but it also delights in God's grace and forgiveness for when we fail.

I realise that there's much more to say on this subject of obedience. There are complex questions about how the Old Testament laws relate to Christians today. There are wonderful treasures to be found in our union with Christ and the way that shapes our understanding of obedience. You will need to read other books on this subject if you want to explore those more, so I have listed a few on page 190.

But in this book I have tried to deliberately focus in on one aspect of our obedience: namely, the reality of obeying God by faith in him rather than confidence in ourselves.

You will know that you are walking this path when you are honest, sorry, dependent and taking action. It will be a tough but deeply joyful road to walk.

This is a lifelong walk. I've found this book pretty tough to write as I have been confronted again and again by my own need to learn these lessons. But I'm hopeful and optimistic. Even in the face of repeated failure, there is power to make progress. That's the life I'm longing to live.

The greatest commandment

When Jesus was asked about the greatest commandment, he gave this reply:

> *"The most important one," answered Jesus, "is this: 'Hear, O Israel: the Lord our God, the Lord is one. Love the Lord your God with all your heart and with all your soul and with all your mind and with all your strength.' The second is this: 'Love your neighbour as yourself.' There is no commandment greater than these."*
>
> *(Mark 12 v 29-31)*

It all boils down to this. Two commandments that sum it all up: love God and love your neighbour.

But Jesus didn't just *give* these two commandments—he also *lived* them. He perfectly loved God and he perfectly loved his neighbour. Jesus lived a perfect life of obedience. Although it's impossible for us, it wasn't for him. He lived it every moment of every day. His obedience was complete, even to death on a cross.

Our hope rests in his perfect obedience. His obedient death saves us from the punishment we deserve.

But not only that. His perfect obedience is also essential for our life of obedience. He has lived it, and, as we trust him, we discover the power to live it.

In this book we've looked at some of the commands we find in the Bible. They're not easy commands. In fact, they're impossible commands. But if you find yourself beginning to sink into despair, please remember that Jesus is our hope. Let your frustration and disappointment keep driving you back to him. Without him we won't make any progress.

This book will have missed the mark if you have got to the end and feel crushed. Please keep remembering that the aim is joyful, humble, Spirit-empowered obedience.

The perfect man

And remember, this is the road that Jesus walked perfectly. He has lived this impossible life. He alone has kept every one of God's good commands. He alone has lived the life of joyful and perfect obedience. He alone has faced temptation and won the battle every time. He alone has dealt with the punishment our sin deserves. And he alone has broken the power of sin for us.

Hope rises within us as we see that Jesus is our King, who goes ahead of us into battle. Our failures no longer need to condemn us. Our weakness no longer needs to crush us. Our fears no longer need to terrify us. And our sin no longer needs to rule us.

When you feel despair, guilt or self-doubt rising within you, don't ignore it and hope it goes away. And don't allow it to dominate and define you. Instead, allow it to drive you to Jesus. He alone is your hope. He has the power to help you change.

So the next time you're reading your Bible or sitting in church or listening to a Christian podcast, and a command comes up that makes you think, "That's impossible!" don't excuse yourself, or redefine the command, or ignore it, or crush yourself.

Instead, look to Jesus. He has already obeyed that command for you. His death has paid for your forgiveness. His obedience has been counted as your obedience. You have nothing to prove—you are already right in God's eyes.

Then approach the command and say, "Yes, it's impossible. I can't. I'm sorry. Please help. Let's go."

Helpful books

Here are some books that will help you to think through what it looks like in practice to live a life of joyful obedience:

- *The Enemy Within* by Kris Lundgaard (published by P&R)

- *You Can Change* by Tim Chester (published by IVP)

- *Sipping Saltwater* by Steve Hoppe (published by The Good Book Company)

Thank you

Thanks so much to my precious church family at The Globe who have listened (perhaps even multiple times) to most of this material being preached. Being a pastor will always come before being a writer, and I count it an enormous privilege to be able to serve you.

Thanks to Alison, who has patiently got this book to the finishing line. Your skill as an editor has vastly improved this book. I thank God for the gifts he has given you.

And thanks to Linda and my three boys. I love that we get to serve Jesus as a team. Let's keep going in joyful obedience to the greatest King.

thegoodbook

COMPANY

BIBLICAL | RELEVANT | ACCESSIBLE

At The Good Book Company, we are dedicated to helping Christians and local churches grow. We believe that God's growth process always starts with hearing clearly what he has said to us through his timeless word—the Bible.

Ever since we opened our doors in 1991, we have been striving to produce Bible-based resources that bring glory to God. We have grown to become an international provider of user-friendly resources to the Christian community, with believers of all backgrounds and denominations using our books, Bible studies, devotionals, evangelistic resources, and DVD-based courses.

We want to equip ordinary Christians to live for Christ day by day, and churches to grow in their knowledge of God, their love for one another, and the effectiveness of their outreach.

Call us for a discussion of your needs or visit one of our local websites for more information on the resources and services we provide.

Your friends at The Good Book Company

thegoodbook.com | thegoodbook.co.uk
thegoodbook.com.au | thegoodbook.co.nz
thegoodbook.co.in